To Jane –
May you always
feel His presence
and joy – He is
faithful!
Jer 29:11

Ashley Graham

Do You
Know Me?

A Revelation of Relationship

Ashley N. Gronholm

WESTBOW
P R E S S°
A DIVISION OF THOMAS NELSON
& ZONDERVAN

WestBow Press books may be ordered through booksellers or by contacting:

WestBow Press
A Division of Thomas Nelson & Zondervan
1663 Liberty Drive
Bloomington, IN 47403
www.westbowpress.com
844-714-3454

ISBN: 979-8-3850-0543-7 (sc)
ISBN: 979-8-3850-0541-3 (hc)
ISBN: 979-8-3850-0542-0 (e)

Library of Congress Control Number: 2023915559

Print information available on the last page.

WestBow Press rev. date: 09/11/2023

This book is dedicated to my darling husband Greg, the love of my life, and to our wonderful children: Natalie, Jacob, Nicole, and Christian.

"It is my great privilege and joy to endorse Ashley Gronholm's book *Do You Know Me?: A Revelation of Relationship*. It has been an honor to associate with Ashley's ministry and hear her testimony of how the Holy Spirit, through grace and truth, rescued her from false beliefs into true revelation and relationship with God.

"The key to demonstrating 'a revelation of relationship' requires a teachable spirit and pure love that draws people to the love of Jesus. Ashley carries this spirit and love, which enables Christ, through her, to compassionately listen to people's real-life stories and transform souls. Her gift of teaching, as demonstrated in *Do You Know Me?: A Revelation of Relationship*, ushers readers into a deeper love with Jesus and equips them to lead others to into Christ's love for eternity."

—**Prakash Daniel**
MA (Biblical Studies), DDiv

"Ashley Gronholm's latest publication, *Do You Know Me?*, offers a revelation of the believer's awesome opportunity of a life-changing and enduring relationship with our heavenly Father. It is written with clarity and deep spiritual insights that the author has personally experienced, and it shows on every page. You will be informed and inspired, but most importantly you will be transformed into a deeper and more joyous relationship with Father God as you apply the eternal trues that Ashley has so capably written in *Do You Know Me*.

—**Dr. Larry Langston**
CEO of Best Life TV

CONTENTS

INTRODUCTION

"Beloved"

Psalm 130:1–7
Lord, I cry out to you out of the depths of my despair!
Hear my voice, O God!
Answer this prayer and hear my plea of mercy.

Lord, if you measured us and marked us with our sins,
who would ever have their prayers answered?

But your forgiving love is what makes you so wonderful.
No wonder you are loved and worshiped!

This is why I wait upon you, expecting your breakthrough,
for your Word brings me hope.

I long for you more than any watchman
would long for the morning light.
I will watch and wait for you, O God,
throughout the night.

O Israel, keep hoping, keep trusting,
and keep waiting on the Lord,
for he is tenderhearted, kind, and forgiving.
He has a thousand ways to set you free![1]

The love and grace of Jesus are *breathtaking*—transforming you from the inside out. When life is spinning out of control and you have no one to turn to and you feel utterly alone in your struggle, pain, and loss, you are on holy ground, for this is the place where you will encounter the love and grace of Jesus, if you will lift your eyes to the heavens and cry out to Jesus.

It was the year of 2010. I was in bed, sick, destitute, abandoned, afraid, betrayed, and alone. I was searching and felt as if I were barely hanging on and at the end of my rope. I never wanted divorce and felt so heartbroken for my three beautiful children, ages sixteen, thirteen, and twelve, who were so vulnerable and in need of stability in life. But regardless of what I wanted, the divorce was happening, and there was no refuge, no comfort, no hope—*only despair and fear.* I was angry, lashing out in rebellion and heading for destruction. My life had become a complicated web of trauma and pain that I knew I would never be able to recover from—*on my own.*

What a strange place to be, considering that I had always wanted to follow God and obey Him. The trouble wasn't a lack of desire, but a lack of knowledge and understanding of the heart of Jesus and His amazing grace and the power of His Holy Spirit. Hosea 4:6 says, "My people are destroyed for lack of knowledge." I did not know the truth of Jesus—that He is one with *God.* This lack of knowledge of the Trinity—Father, Son, and Holy Spirit as one—limited my ability to walk in the *true* grace, victory, and authority of Jesus Christ. People do the strangest things when they don't know that their true identity is rooted in the love of God, who is *Jesus Christ.* I was searching for love, but I did not have a clue where true love comes from until I encountered the love and grace of Jesus, who set me free.

In the midnight hour of my life, I encountered love, mercy, and grace in my time of need because Jesus heard my cry and He came for me—*He rescued me!* All my life, I had a "head knowledge" of Jesus, but I didn't really have a sense of His abounding love and grace. I call that kind of knowledge a "heart knowledge." This is what was missing from my life: the heart of Jesus and His amazing grace. We don't encounter the grace of Jesus until our midnight hour, when we've exhausted every other possible option and come up empty-handed. This is the place where all ideologies, philosophies, and beliefs collide with the penetrating, transforming power of the love and grace of Jesus—if we are willing to cry out for help and be healed.

My problem was that I had lived a self-righteous life of self-sufficiency and religion and believed that I had everything I needed to go to heaven after this life. But being "born again" or "saved" wasn't in my repertoire. Why? I was living under the false assumption that I didn't need saving because I believed I had everything I needed, *as long as* ...

Let's dial in on that phrase, "as long as." In my life, it manifested in the following ways: "As long as I keep all the commandments." "As long as I obey perfectly." "As long as I am faithful." "As long as I endure to the end." The phrase "as long as" implies contingency. In other words, I was living in a belief system that had embedded religious lies deep inside my heart and mind, enslaving my spirit. What was the lie? The lie was the belief that my position in heaven, meaning where I would end up spending all eternity, was *contingent upon my choice to obey Mormon teachings, doctrines, and scripture.* Within Mormonism, Jesus is a mere brother and not one with God. He is a mere "sacrificial lamb" who made it possible for human beings to one day become "gods." This is not what the Bible teaches. But how was I to know that, given that I was born into a Mormon family and was a direct descendent of one of the original twelve apostles of the Mormon Church?

I am grateful to say that I am alive and still standing today because of the powerful way Jesus delivered me from the bondage of false religion into the Kingdom of His Son! I witness to you today that the authority and power of the love and grace of Jesus Christ are strong enough to break any chain, free any captive, and heal all brokenness, for Jesus came to set the captive *free*. In my critical hour, I was facing a crisis of faith, because during my divorce, as I experienced rejection, slander, false accusations, and betrayal from every side, my belief system began to crumble like a sandcastle on the shore; it was washing away before my very eyes. The horror, fear, and despair I felt during that season of my life are indescribable! There was nothing I could do to stop the erosion of the waves from carrying away all my hopes and dreams into a vast, dark, icy sea.

There is a picture of Jesus portrayed in a photography book that I absolutely love. The book is "Journeys with the Messiah" by J. Michael Belk, a very gifted and anointed artist and a personal friend of mine. In this picture, Jesus is depicted walking out over the sea holding a life preserver. In the background is a sinking rowboat. The caption below the image reads: "Only a fool would go to sea without a Life Savior."[2] The truth is this: we can't make it through this life without a real "life savior." Jesus Christ, who is one with the Father and the Holy Spirit, is our true savior, Yeshua, the God who saves. But having not known this truth in my spirit at the time of my divorce, I underwent a season of deep testing and trial. I can remember collapsing on my bed numerous times a day and just sobbing. I would cry until I couldn't cry anymore, and then I would drag myself out of bed to try to take care of my children and make it through the rest of the day. Looking back, I can see that Jesus was with me the whole time, preparing my heart for the moment He would set me free. It's beautiful to me that Jesus doesn't force Himself on us but allows us to walk long enough in our pain to be ready to reach out to Him—to cry out for rescue.

In my darkest hour, about a year into my divorce, after attending a Christian church for that time, I heard the message of grace: unmerited favor from God when you least deserve it. I desperately longed to know Jesus from the perspective of grace rather than from the burden of striving to earn His love. From the depths of my soul, I cried out to God, asking if grace was a real thing and not some fairy-tale, cure-all, or "fix." I knew I was wading in deep icy waters and wasn't going to be able to make it to shore on my own. I needed rescuing. It was a *critical* hour of my life—the midnight hour. In this moment, I lifted up my prayer: "Is this 'grace' a real thing? Because if it is, I need some grace."

It was in that moment of seeking to understand grace, out of the deepest longing of my heart, that I encountered the love and grace of Jesus! Truly, the grace of Jesus turned the key to my prison cell and set me free. It's not easy to describe what occurred next, and for a long time, I didn't fully understand it. The supernatural, unfathomable love and grace of God is by nature indescribable. It's good for it to be so; otherwise, we

---

2   J. Michael Belk, *Life Savior*, in "Journeys with the Messiah: A Fashion Photographer Explores the Modern-Day Relevance of Jesus" (Brentwood Press, 2017).

would not desire to seek it for ourselves. One thing is for sure: Jesus met me in my seeking, and I encountered *Him*. I can hear you asking, "What was it like to encounter the love of Jesus?" Honestly, there are no words to begin to explain it. All I can say is that I felt deeply loved, whole, healed, forgiven, redeemed, and set free! The experience lasted for hours as I wept and wept and wept. There was a rolling sensation or movement deep in my belly, filling me with indescribable joy. That day, a lifetime of burdens were lifted as I experienced what it means to truly be loved. That day, Jesus called me His beloved, and He became my beloved.

Jesus is now and forevermore the lover of my *soul*. Truly, the love and grace of Jesus set me free from a thousand heartbreaks, a thousand horrors, a thousand betrayals, and a thousand fears. He is El Shaddai, Mashiach, Adonai, Rapha, God Almighty, Messiah, Master, Healer. Jesus has a thousand ways to set you free!

Even to this day, I continue to rest in the amazing love and grace of Jesus. Sometimes I am tempted to fall back into striving and performing. Jesus has been faithful to me in my struggle and continues to speak the words "Be still" over my spirit. Jesus is faithful and true. He is God, and He loves you with an unfailing love. He says to you, "Come! You are Mine."

I am a songwriter, and as I look back over my life, I see the grace of Jesus wooing me to Him through Holy Spirit–breathed lyrics. In 2008 I wrote a song called "I Am Yours." Revel with me for a moment in the prophetic word given to me that prophesied of my own future moment when Jesus would set me free a little over a year later:

I Am Yours

Even when the darker side drowns out the light
Even when my wandering soul refuses to do right
I know you will never give up the fight
For I am YOURS.
I am YOURS and YOU are MINE
And with your BLOOD you paid the PRICE
And you will never let me go
Even when I put up a fight.
For I am Yours.

ONE

Do You Trust Me?

Trust in the LORD with all thine heart; and lean
not unto thine own understanding.
—Proverbs 3:5

Proverbs 16:3 tells us that when we choose to trust God, He will establish our plans. I believe it is true that God always has a good plan for our lives and will go before us to prepare a way for us to encounter His love. However, along the way, we may experience setbacks, failure, or lost time. It is never God's intention to disqualify, distract, or delay our destiny! The truth is that our sovereign God has allowed His plan to unfold throughout time, turning all things for good for those who love God and are called according to His purpose (Romans 8:28). We see this biblical truth powerfully displayed in the life, death, and resurrection of Jesus Christ, who came to set the captives free (Isaiah 61:1–7).

Years ago, I entered a difficult season of life and found myself totally depleted emotionally, physically, and spiritually. During this time, by the power of the Holy Spirit, I came to the revelation that placing my faith in Jesus Christ alone was the key to experiencing true freedom and joy! I received the truth that I could not truly *know* Jesus without a personal relationship with Him. I am not talking about religion or a "head knowledge" of Jesus combined with ritualistic rule keeping. I am speaking of relationship—an intimate, passionate love for Jesus, who is the Bridegroom (John 3:29; Revelation 19:7) and the lover of our souls. By His grace and power, I discovered that as I fully surrendered my life to Jesus Christ, I was set free from fear, shame, condemnation, failure, and a lack of purpose. This is why I now believe that when we encounter the love and grace of Jesus Christ as our personal Lord and Savior, we will find our true identity and discover our purpose: to live for Jesus Christ and *be free!*

Looking back, I can clearly see that when life began spinning out of control, I did not know Jesus the way I am describing Him to you now. Nevertheless, it was in that fire of the furnace of testing that I encountered the love, grace, mercy, and power of Jesus Christ and was supernaturally set free. Jesus filled me with His love and power, healing me from the inside out, and I have never been the same. This supernatural encounter with Jesus Christ, by the power of the Holy Spirit, released a process of purification and sanctification, leading to a complete personal life transformation!

Today I have come to know that our victory in the Christian life is all about relationship with Jesus, who is the "living water" and the "bread of life" (John 4:10; John 6:35). One of my favorite stories in scripture is of Mary Magdalene. She was abused and possessed by demons, likely living the life of a prostitute. She was violated and broken in every way a woman can be. How do I know? Scripture tells us that Jesus cast seven demons out of her! Jesus clearly gave an astounding response to this woman, who was despised by the religious leaders of her day. "Wherefore I say unto thee, Her sins, which are many, are forgiven; for she loved much: but to whom little is forgiven, the same loveth little" (Luke 7:47). From this encounter with Jesus, Mary went on to become one of His most loyal and devoted followers and was even the first to see Jesus when He rose from the dead!

The story of Mary Magdalene's conversion is a beautiful model for us to look to when considering the power of placing our faith in Jesus Christ. When we are in relationship with Jesus Christ as a result of being rescued from our sin, shame, and condemnation, we cannot help but want to worship Him for who *He* is: King of kings and Lord of lords! From this place in the Spirit, religious ritual and a list of "shoulds" in our lives can be transformed into a desire to serve the Lord because we *want* to—not because we feel obligated to. When we encounter the true love of Jesus, we become lovers of Him, and it becomes our joy and passion to serve Him with our whole hearts! Psalm 37:4 (NKJV) tells us, "Delight yourself also in the LORD, and He shall give you the desires of your heart." Maybe this seems hard for some to believe, but when I experienced the indescribable love, grace, mercy, and power of Jesus Christ through the power of the Holy Spirit, all my fear, anxiety, torment, doubt, unbelief, and shame were *gone*, and in their place was a new joy unspeakable! Wouldn't you like to experience deep, lasting joy and be free of emotional, mental, spiritual, and physical pain? Isaiah 61:1–3, 7 tells us more about all the benefits of knowing Jesus that would flow to us out of His ministry to the brokenhearted:

> The Spirit of the Lord GOD is upon me; because the LORD hath anointed me to preach good tidings unto the meek; he hath sent me to bind up the brokenhearted, to proclaim liberty to the captives, and the opening of the prison to them that are bound; to proclaim the acceptable year of the LORD, and the day of vengeance of our God; to comfort all that mourn; to appoint unto them that mourn in Zion, to give unto them beauty for ashes, the oil of joy for mourning, the garment of praise for the spirit of heaviness; that they might be called trees of righteousness, the planting of the LORD, that he might be glorified ... For your shame you shall have double; and for confusion they shall rejoice in their portion: therefore in their land they shall possess the double: everlasting joy shall be unto them.

About a year after my encounter with the Lord, I began to meditate in prayer and memorized this passage of scripture from Isaiah 61. I truly desired to see all the promises listed in Isaiah 61 come forth in my own life! One day at a time, one prayer at a time, one tear at a time, my relationship with Jesus deepened. No longer was I as concerned about whether I had accomplished a certain religious task or rule; I was instead focused on developing a relationship of knowing Jesus and being known by Him! This pursuit of Jesus and an intimate relationship with

Him turned into a deeply satisfying connection through the Holy Spirit that began to yield the sweetest spiritual fruit I had ever known. Truly, I was captivated by the lover of my soul; Jesus, my Bridegroom and King, was lavishing me with His love—and He is still lavishing me today!

This daily pursuit of Jesus through an intimate relationship with Him led to an impactful understanding of how to *trust* Jesus. After all, cultivating a relationship with anyone takes effort, doesn't it? So that is what I did. I was so hungry for truth from God's Word, healing from my past, and comfort to get through the day that at first light, right when I woke up every day, I would almost run to my special room—my own personal "upper room" (Mark 14:15; Acts 1:13–14)—and seek His face! What did this look like in practical terms? I would turn on soft, calming, hymn-themed music, pop up my feet on a couch, and get comfortable. Then I would close my eyes and begin to allow the worship music to wash over my spirit as I soaked in His presence. Then I would journal what I saw as the Holy Spirit revealed images, thoughts, or impressions. Next I would hold my Bible close to my heart and pray for the Lord Himself to speak to me through His Word! Ten years later, without fail, I have encountered the Lord in worship daily, and I hear His voice while enjoying His many benefits because I choose to seek His face in the "secret place." What is the "secret place"? It is a place of rest in the spiritual realm of God's holiness and presence, where your heart encounters God's heart through a surrendered relationship with Jesus Christ by the power of the Holy Spirit. "He that dwelleth in the secret place of the most High shall abide under the shadow of the Almighty" (Psalm 91:1).

Here, in the secret place, or in relationship with Jesus, I can be hidden away in the comforting arms of Jesus. Here I can simply give myself permission to rest in knowing that Jesus is my defender who will come to me and rescue me from all my battles.

This is my heart's desire for this book: to awaken you to the reality that you, too, can encounter Jesus and His love for you daily as you develop a personal relationship with Him. The mission and purpose of Be Free Ministry, the ministry the Lord led me to create twelve years ago, is to help broken people encounter the love, grace, and mercy of Jesus Christ by the power of the Holy Spirit, and be set free![3]

---

[3] For more information about Be Free Ministry, visit www.BeFreeInChrist Ministry.org.

Every human being knows suffering. We can choose to focus our attention on all the wrongs and injustices that have occurred and remain bitter, angry, and wounded, or we can choose to receive the good news of Jesus Christ and be healed in every possible way! We can finally take the first step when we realize that we can *choose* to trust God. We do not have to be victims; we can choose to be overcomers! If you are ready to take that first step of faith, your transformation from suffering and pain to joy and healing can begin! Or if you've known about Jesus for many years but are wrestling with lukewarm faith, today is the perfect time to take that first step and begin to entrust your life to Jesus, who laid down His life for us so we could be healed, whole, and free.

It is my most sincere prayer for you that today you will accept this invitation to know Jesus in a personal and powerful way. Let's start that journey toward healing and joy today.

Jesus is waiting for you to call His name!

TWO

Encountering the Love of Jesus

And he said, The God of our fathers hath chosen thee, that
thou shouldest know his will, and see that Just One, and
shouldest hear the voice of his mouth. For thou shalt be his
witness unto all men of what thou hast seen and heard.
—Acts 22:14–15

E ven though I spent the first half of my life hearing of and learning about Jesus within the walls of a church, looking back on it now, I can honestly tell you that I did not truly know this Jesus that I am describing to you today. I knew of Jesus but had not yet entered into a fully surrendered relationship with Jesus. I did not fully understand what it meant to submit my life to God's will, and in many ways, I was living life to please myself. If you had asked me back then whether I believed in Jesus, I would most certainly have said, "Yes, of course!" However, believing in Jesus and knowing Jesus are not the same thing! Up to that point in life, at age thirty-eight, I had kept all the religious rules I knew of, but my heart was full of resentment, frustration, fear, and malice from abuse. I was exhausted from ministry burnout and from trying to please a works-based, demanding, and oppressive group of people. In some ways, I was like a Pharisee, one of the religious leaders in the Bible, relying on my ability to obey God's law as the guarantee of my entrance to heaven. "Grace," as I now understand it—a free gift of undeserved merit or favor—was not even a word in my religious vocabulary! Grace simply was not spoken of in my church community and wasn't a part of their doctrine. Granted, in the last decade, I have noticed that the leaders in my former faith have attempted to adopt the concept of grace and incorporate it into their teaching. The trouble is that you can't give away what you don't have!

As I previously stated, I was raised in the Mormon religion, in which grace was offered only *after* a person had done all he or she could do to follow God and obey Him as perfectly as possible. In other words, "grace," in Mormonism, is still works-based! I now know that grace is not grace if it's about earning rewards for good behavior; grace is a free pardon for a sinful heart. The problem with works-based behavior, in which a believer attempts to earn God's love, is that people learn to rely on themselves and their own self-discipline and performance to keep themselves in a "right standing" with God. That is a lot of pressure! The funny thing is, despite all my best efforts, I still couldn't keep the law *perfectly!* Eventually I fell flat on my face in life, and it ended up being the best thing that ever happened to me, because that was when I encountered the love, grace, and power of Jesus. Hallelujah!

I can't rejoice enough in the goodness of our God, who picks us up when we fall down! When we find ourselves deep in a pit and unable to climb out, Jesus doesn't say, "Well, your sin put you in that pit, so figure out how to climb up out of there, and when you do, I will forgive and restore you." *No!* The Jesus I now know will meet you in the middle of your mess and will restore you! He will climb right into that pit with you *and lift you out* because that is the way of His love. It's up to us whether we choose to receive His love and allow His love to change us, or whether we want to still be prideful and stubborn, rejecting His love.

Relationship Reveals Your Identity

Scripture tells us of a man named Paul, who wrote more than half of the New Testament. Paul was never spoken of in my church during all my years of being a Mormon. He was literally *never* mentioned! Now, I was very devoted to the church I was raised in, attending church every Wednesday and Sunday, holding leadership positions, and I was a seminary graduate. If the church taught about Paul, I would know! But church leaders never spoke of Paul, or Saul of Tarsus, as he was formerly known (Acts 9:11, see also Acts 13:9). After becoming an evangelical Christian, I realized that my former church did not even believe that Paul is an apostle! But after studying the Bible on average for five hours a day for the past decade and graduating from a Christian seminary, I can state with the utmost confidence that Paul was in fact *an apostle of Jesus Christ.* How do I know? It is clearly laid out in scripture!

In Acts 22, Paul states that he was a religious Pharisee being prepared to become a rabbi, or a Jewish teacher. He had permission from Caiaphas, the Jewish high priest, to capture, imprison and even kill Christians in an effort to extinguish the Christian movement that was rapidly growing after the crucifixion and resurrection of Jesus Christ. But something very important and unexpected happened to Paul that changed his life forever. As he was embarking on a mission to annihilate Christians, Paul had a face-to-face encounter with Jesus Christ Himself on the road to Damascus that changed *everything!*

> I am verily a man which am a Jew, born in Tarsus, a city in Cilicia, yet brought up in this city at the feet of Gamaliel, and taught according to the perfect manner of the law of the fathers, and was zealous toward God, as ye all are this day. And I persecuted this way unto the death, binding and delivering into prisons both men and women. As also the high priest doth bear me witness, and all the estate of the elders: from whom also I received letters unto the brethren, and went to Damascus, to bring them which were there bound unto Jerusalem, for to be punished. And it came to pass, that, as I made my journey, and was come nigh unto Damascus about noon, suddenly there shone from heaven a great light round about me. And I fell unto the ground, and heard a voice saying unto me, Saul, Saul, why persecutes thou me? And I answered, Who art thou, Lord? And he said unto me, I am Jesus of Nazareth, whom thou persecutest. And they that were with me saw indeed the light, and were afraid; but they heard not the voice of him that spake to me. And I said, What shall I do, Lord? And the Lord

said unto me, Arise, and go into Damascus; and there it shall be told thee of all things which are appointed for thee to do. And when I could not see for the glory of that light, being led by the hand of them that were with me, I came into Damascus. And one Ananias, a devout man according to the law, having a good report of all the Jews which dwelt there, came unto me, and stood, and said unto me, Brother Saul, receive thy sight. And the same hour I looked up upon him. And he said, The God of our fathers hath chosen thee, that thou shouldest know his will, and see that Just One, and shouldest hear the voice of his mouth. For thou shalt be his witness unto all men of what thou hast seen and heard. And now why tarriest thou? arise, and be baptized, and wash away thy sins, calling on the name of the Lord. (Acts 22:3–16)

This powerful testimony of Paul's conversion is an example of how each of us can encounter Jesus Christ. Despite all of Paul's sin, Jesus knew who Paul was from the foundation of the world and had a destiny for him to fulfill. In other words, Jesus had a call on Paul's life, and Paul didn't even know it until he encountered Jesus on the road to Damascus in the middle of his sin and rebellion. The most beautiful part of the story is this: once Paul encountered Jesus, he was awakened to his true destiny, life calling, and purpose! As a result, everything Paul knew was changed, and he was never the same. That is the power of an authentic, chain-breaking, heart-purifying, Holy Spirit–anointing encounter with the heart of God—*Jesus Christ!*

So what about you? Have you ever thought to ask God what His purpose is for *your* life? Scripture tells us that God uniquely created each one of us with a specific purpose in mind and that He foreknew us from before the foundation of the world (Romans 8:28–29; 1 Corinthians 12:18–20; Ephesians 2:10)! If you do not know His purpose for your life, how about asking Jesus? He tells us He is standing at the door of your heart, waiting and knocking (Revelation 3:20). He wants to show His plans and purposes for your life, but first you must let Him in! And the good news is, it isn't hard to do just that! All you need to do is simply ask Jesus in the sincerity of your heart to come to you and show you His plan for your life, and be willing to submit your plans under His lordship and direction. If you truly pray this request in faith, Jesus will come! How do I know? Because He did it for me! Yes, Jesus came to me in my hour of "crying out" to Him, just as He promised He would: "I will not leave you comfortless: I will come to you." (John 14:18)

It is very important to me to share this story with you, not only for the powerful testimony it is of the transforming power of Jesus Christ, but also because I too had a life-changing encounter with the love, grace, and mercy of Jesus Christ, which was a total game-changer! Like Paul, I was in deep rebellion and sin and was all tangled up in misguided "righteous indignation." But Jesus knew how to reach me in that place of confusion and pain and set me free! How did He know? The Word of God says that Jesus, who is one with the Father (John 10:30), foreknew us, chose us, and predestined us from before the foundation of the world to hear the voice of God and follow Him:

> Paul, an apostle of Jesus Christ by the will of God, to the saints which are at Ephesus, and to the faithful in Christ Jesus: Grace be to you, and peace, from God our Father, and from the Lord Jesus Christ. Blessed be the God and Father of our Lord Jesus Christ, who hath blessed us with all spiritual blessings in heavenly places in Christ: According as he hath chosen[4] us in him before the foundation of the world,[5] that we should be holy and without blame before him in love: Having predestined us[6] unto the adoption[7] of children by Jesus Christ to himself, according to the good pleasure of his

---

[4] See Romans 8:28: "And we know that all things work together for good to them that love God, to them who are the called according to *his* purpose."

[5] See 1 Peter 1:2: "Elect according to the foreknowledge of God the Father, through sanctification of the Spirit, unto obedience and sprinkling of the blood of Jesus Christ: Grace unto you, and peace, be multiplied."

[6] See Acts 13:48: "And when the Gentiles heard this, they were glad, and glorified the word of the Lord: and as many as were ordained to eternal life believed."

[7] See John 1:12: "But as many as received him, to them gave he power to become the sons of God, *even* to them that believe on his name."

will,[8] To the praise of the glory of his grace, wherein he hath made us accepted in the beloved. In whom we have redemption through his blood,[9] the forgiveness of sins, according to the riches of his grace. (Ephesians 1:1–7)

Here we see truth laid out clearly in scripture, revealing our true identity through a relationship with Jesus Christ as our Lord and Savior! This revelation of identity in Christ is exactly what occurred in Paul's life! He thought he was destined to become a Jewish rabbi and believed he had a mandate from God to imprison, torture, and allow Christians to be killed. But when Paul encountered Jesus Christ Himself on the road to Damascus and was struck blind for three days, God sent a believer named Ananias, who was anointed with the power of God through the infilling of the Holy Spirit, to lay hands on Paul and heal him (Acts 9). This miraculous healing then enabled Paul to fulfill the mission, or purpose, God had for him through believing in and obeying Jesus Christ. What happened to Paul was no small thing. In fact, Paul had experienced a miracle encounter with Jesus Christ that changed his life forever.

I want the world to know that Paul's story is my story—and it can be everyone's story if people will open their hearts to the truth that a personal encounter with Jesus Christ is real and possible! I would never have believed it were possible until an encounter with the love and grace of Jesus Christ actually happened to me.

So what *exactly* am I saying? I am saying that, for several hours, while alone in my bed reading about the grace of Jesus Christ, I released a cry from my heart to my heavenly Father, asking whether this "grace message" was true or just a bunch of lies. In a time of life crisis, I found myself a year into my divorce, and my life had become a living nightmare. Failure was staring me down in the mirror every day, and the

---

[8]   See 1 Corinthians 1:21: "For after that in the wisdom of God the world by wisdom knew not God, it pleased God by the foolishness of preaching to save them that believe."

[9]   See Hebrews 9:12: "Neither by the blood of goats and calves, but by his own blood he entered in once into the holy place, having obtained eternal redemption for us."

agony was crushing! I didn't know whether I would survive it all, and I really mean that—I did not know if I was strong enough to survive what was happening to me. I was experiencing daily emotional breakdowns where I would fall on the floor and sob and sob and sob! This moment in time felt like life or death, and I felt like I was losing the battle, as though my life was literally hanging in the balance. Have you ever felt as if everything you had believed about your life and belief system was suddenly in question? That's where I was, and I found myself struggling to find my way through a very complicated web of lies. I was experiencing rejection on every side, and all my relationships became strained or were eliminated, including those with my closest friends, my family, and even some of my children for a season. I literally felt as if I were losing my mind! I felt I had nowhere to turn. Then I met *Jesus!*

When I encountered Jesus Christ by His grace and the power of the Holy Spirit, I experienced an inexplicable, massive tidal wave of love poured out over my spirit, mind, and body that no human words can describe. I felt completely and totally held in a state of extreme peace, joy, comfort, and love! I was so overwhelmed that all I could do was lie in bed and weep. I experienced indescribable joy and peace beyond comprehension. It was like an out-of-body experience where I was aware that something was taking place in me but I wasn't the one making it happen. What do I mean? I was lying in bed, but I couldn't hold still! God's power came upon me, and I could feel Him moving through my body. At times, I would cough violently. I believe demons were leaving my body as the Holy Spirit ministered to me. I know now that what I experienced was a very powerful healing and a spiritual deliverance. Truly Jesus poured His love over me, and those demons had to flee!

After the Spirit of the Lord came upon me with power, I went into a deep state of rest and slept for almost twenty-four hours. When I awoke the next day, I was amazed at how rested and fresh I felt in my body, mind, and spirit! I felt completely *changed*, and in fact I *was* changed: I had been filled with the power of God, and I had been born again. I immediately knew in the deepest depths of my spirit that I could no longer live my life the way I had before and that change was ahead. I also began to discern with new spiritual wisdom from heaven and had greater clarity about what changes needed to be made in my life, and I began to implement them. This wasn't easy, because it meant disappointing certain people who had become very important to me, and it meant closing the door to some dreams that I had invested many years in pursuing—in particular, a musical career. I had already written, recorded, and produced four full-length CDs and had just released my first international Nashville single. But I knew I was being called to obey Jesus and serve Him, which would require a "dying to self" in which I laid down my former dreams to pursue more of Jesus. Now, looking back on it all, I can powerfully testify that the Lord has blessed my life beyond my wildest dreams and has given me back one hundredfold what I had lost!

I am sharing this story with you because my encounter with Jesus was so life-altering that it became the catalyst for establishing Be Free Ministry: to help people encounter the love and grace of Jesus Christ through the power of the Holy Spirit and be set free from their past regrets, spiritual strongholds and false religion. The Apostle Paul's encounter with Jesus on the road to Damascus is important to me because I identify with it personally. It is my desire to help others receive the truth that they, too, can have a "road to Damascus" encounter with Jesus Christ that can change their lives forever and reveal their destiny and purpose! In fact, I am certain of it after watching it happen right before my eyes over and over again during our encounter retreats for women in the beautiful mountains of Ellijay, Georgia![10] After facilitating twenty women's retreats and over thirty prayer retreats for men and women, I now know with certainty that if you are hungry for God and seek Him with all your heart, you will find Him! My husband Greg and I, together with our faithful ministry team of volunteers, have offered women's retreats with worship, prayer, and Bible-based teaching since 2015. If you are reading this as a skeptic, not sure if you can trust what I am telling you, just know that I get it and I understand. It can be hard to believe when life has been full of lies, disappointment, and pain. Can I make a suggestion? Perhaps you could pray a simple prayer with me. Just one simple prayer of faith can move mountains of unbelief and doubt! Shall we try?

---

[10] To know more about Be Free Ministry Retreats, visit www.BeFreeInChrist Ministry.org.

Heavenly Father, I believe You love me and that You want to heal me and set me free from fear, shame, condemnation, and sin. I believe you sent your son Jesus Christ to suffer and die for me. I ask you to touch my broken heart with Your love. I've been hurt, and I am tired and broken and want to be free. Today, I choose to forgive everyone who has hurt me, knowing that you allowed your Son Jesus to die for my sins so I could be forgiven. Today, I choose to place my faith in Jesus Christ so I can be set free from my regret, fear, anxiety and sin and experience Your love, grace, and power! Today, I choose to surrender my life to Jesus Christ, and invite Him to come into my life and be my Lord and Savior, in Jesus Name, Amen.

This is my prayer: that every person living on this planet would come to know and love Jesus Christ and makes Him the Lord of his or her life! Like the woman who reached out and touched the hem of Jesus's robe and was healed (Luke 8:40–48), you, too, can be healed— just like that! Let my life be living proof! After my personal encounter with Jesus, I was physically, emotionally, mentally, and spiritually healed in an instant! I was supernaturally healed of three autoimmune diseases, trauma, and bitterness beyond comprehension. What made it happen? I simply asked, "God, is your grace actually real?" I didn't ask this question lightly; I really wanted an answer, and Jesus knew I had reached the end of my rope and that my heart was ready to receive His love.

But before the healing came, I heard a question that resounded in my spirit: "Will you forgive the ones who have hurt you the most?" I paused for a moment on that thought. I had been listening to the gospel message in a Christian church for about a year. I was skeptical. I had my doubts. I was afraid of God's punishment and did not know how to comprehend the meaning of grace as it had been newly explained to me. Could grace truly be enough to save me? Could God really forgive my sins without my having a proven track record of consistent good behavior? Was God really that good and kind? Finally, I concluded that I simply could no longer tolerate life as I knew it. I had to know if what I had been told about grace was true. I no longer wanted any deception in my life-- I only wanted *truth*. It was in that moment that I released the answer to God: *Yes, I choose to forgive those who have harmed me.* It was in that very moment of choice that something very supernatural occurred. I am not able to put into words how I felt as the love of God poured over me from heaven. I can say that I was completely overwhelmed and undone by the mercy of God. Tears of pain, disappointment, agony, fear, regret, and loss were transformed into awe, wonder, joy, and peace! I literally experienced in real time what I believe Jesus told us He came to do for us: to heal our broken hearts. Isaiah 61:1–3 perfectly describes what Jesus has done for me—and what He wants to do for you!

> The Spirit of the Lord GOD is upon me; because the LORD hath anointed me to preach good tidings unto the meek; he hath sent me to bind up the brokenhearted, to proclaim liberty to the captives, and the opening of the prison to them that are bound; To proclaim the acceptable year of the LORD, and the day of vengeance of our God; to comfort all that mourn; To appoint unto them that mourn in Zion, to give unto them beauty for ashes, the oil of joy for mourning, the garment of paise for the spirit of heaviness; that they might be called trees of righteousness, the planting of the LORD, that he might be glorified.

Jesus came to heal our hearts from the pain of this life and set us free. Instead of mourning, He will give you joy. Instead of ashes, He will give you beauty. Instead of living a life bound to sin, He will set you free! In my hour of healing, Jesus looked on my heart and knew I was ready to receive His love. I want to encourage you today; truly, it's never too late to put your trust in Jesus and be set free!

It is my prayer that you will choose to rest in the love of Jesus today. If you will simply invite Jesus to be the Lord of your life, He will come to you and heal you right now—just come as you are! Jesus has promised in His Word that He will never leave you or forsake you

(Deuteronomy 31:6). If you have surrendered your life to Jesus, your eternal life of joy and salvation has begun. Welcome into the family of God! Today is the beginning of your best life, because you have placed your faith in Jesus Christ and have believed the testimony of the life of Jesus Christ—that He died for your sins, rose from the grave on the third day, defeated death and hell, ascended back to the Father, and is now in heaven, interceding for *you* and me! No amount of personal effort, striving, or good works will *earn* you a place in heaven. Only by the finished work of Jesus Christ are we truly saved. Believing by faith, you are now a member of God's family and an heir to His eternal promises for you in heaven. Hallelujah!

You Can Be Free!

Remember: joy in our journey here in this life is all about living *in relationship with Jesus Christ.* This is my whole purpose in writing this book: to help you desire to know Jesus and live being loved by Him. How wonderful it is that we can not only know *about* Jesus but can also enjoy a life-transforming personal relationship *with* Him! When we choose to trust Jesus, we allow Him to take away the sting and pain of sin and failure so that His love, mercy, and grace can fill us with His power through the Holy Spirit. This is how you can be set free and can begin to enjoy a personal, intimate, life-giving, transforming relationship with Him. I can personally testify that Jesus entered into that deep, dark pit I was in and lifted me up and out and placed my feet on the rock of His salvation! What a blessed journey it has been to fall head over heels in love with Jesus every day. This is my most sincere desire for anyone who is searching for purpose in life. Only when we know Jesus will we find truth and rest. There is no self-help book, no program, no conference, no church, and no amount of money or fame that could ever compare to the powerful life-giving benefits of a personal relationship with Jesus Christ and the infilling and sealing power of the Holy Spirit.

What about you? Are you ready to truly know Jesus? Perhaps you took a leap of faith and you gave your heart to Jesus while reading this book. If you did, a celebration is in order, for Jesus and all the hosts of heaven are rejoicing over you! "I say unto you, that likewise joy shall be in heaven over one sinner that repenteth, more than over ninety and none just persons, which need no repentance" (Luke 15:7). The New American Standard Bible 1995 (NASB1995) says it this way: "I tell you that in the same way, there will be more joy in heaven over one sinner who repents than over ninety-nine righteous persons who need no repentance" (Luke 15:7).

If you have repented of your sins and asked Jesus to heal you, you are on your path to freedom! For those of you who placed your faith in Jesus years ago and have not found the freedom and joy you had hoped for and find that you've grown distant or cold—not because Jesus's love has withdrawn from *you*, but because you've grown weary—I want to encourage you to continue and not give up! Scripture says it this way: "And let us not be weary in well doing: for in due season we shall reap, if we faint not"[11] (Galatians 6:9).

Let's be honest, this life can be messy and painful. Perhaps you tried to put your faith and trust in Jesus and things just didn't seem to work out the way you had hoped. I know how you feel, because I've been there! But, praise Jesus, I am on the other side of that valley, and I can witness with complete assurance that you can absolutely trust Jesus with your life, because Jesus will *never* fail you. The trouble is not with Jesus and His faithfulness, but with us and our lack of faith. Sometimes we have expectations, and when those expectations for our lives do not appear to be met, we can be tempted to assume that it is because Jesus didn't hear our prayers—or worse, that He chose not to answer them. I've come through so many horrific trials—too many to write of in this book—and I can witness with total assurance that Jesus loves you and knows you by name! He has heard your prayers, and He has not forgotten you! Jesus tells us in His Word that He cares for us and will answer us when we call out to Him: "I will not leave you comfortless: I will come to you" (John 14:18).

Jesus is with you and is very near to the brokenhearted (Psalm 34:18). In fact, Jesus wants a deep and personal relationship with you. We have seen in scripture that Jesus promises to turn all things for our

---

[11]   NKJV: "if we do not lose heart."

good if we love Him and are called to follow Him. Let's take a deeper look at Romans 8:28 and the cross references that come from it:

> And we know that all things work together for good to them that love God, to them who are the called according to his purpose. (Romans 8:28)

> Who hath saved us, and called us with a holy calling, not according to our works, but according to his own purpose and grace, which was given us in Christ Jesus before the world began. (2 Timothy 1:9)[12]

> According as he hath chosen us in him before the foundation of the world, that we should be holy and without blame before him in love. (Ephesians 1:4)

How glorious it is that God's love and grace position us to be declared "holy and without blame," fully able to stand before God, unashamed and loved! Only the love of God could produce the miracle of salvation in the life of a sinner who chooses to believe by faith! God not only declares us righteous, but He also declares that we are "chosen" as His "elect," and He sanctifies us through the Holy Spirit and the blood of Jesus Christ: "Elect according to the foreknowledge of God the Father, through sanctification of the Spirit, unto obedience and sprinkling of the blood of Jesus Christ: Grace unto you, and peace, be multiplied" (1 Peter 1:2).[13]

The reality is this: Jesus desires a personal relationship with you that will break the chains of sin and shame and set you free! The heart of Jesus is to usher you into an authentic personal relationship with Him by the power of the Holy Spirit, that is based not upon works or performance but on trusting that *He is enough!*

---

[12] See Titus 1:2: "In hope of eternal life, which God, that cannot lie, promised before the world began ..."

[13] See Romans 1:7: "To all that be in Rome, beloved of God, called *to be* saints: Grace to you and peace from God our Father, and the Lord Jesus Christ."

THREE

A Hope and a Future!

"For I know the plans I have for you," declares the
LORD, "plans to prosper you and not to harm you,
plans to give you hope and a future."[14]
—Jeremiah 29:11

J esus has a plan. It is just that simple. Choosing to trust His plan, well, that's another story! We don't come out of the womb submitting to Jesus; just the opposite is true. One decision at a time, we come closer to or move farther away from a life-giving relationship with Jesus. The good news is that Jesus has known this from the beginning and established a wonderful plan to set us free from our sins, failures, and chaos! At fifty years old, I have come to know and believe that Jesus is my deliverer because He has delivered me from my own poor choices and the poor choices of others over and over again! Truly, I have come to believe that if we choose to trust Jesus with all our hearts, He will direct our paths!

This "trusting faith" becomes a reality when we begin to realize that God actually has a destiny for our lives and plans for us that are good! God wants to bless and prosper you and has the ability to turn all the bad things that have occurred in your life for your good—if you will trust Him. Romans 8:28 reads, "And we know that all things work together for good to them that love God, to them who are *the called* according

---

[14] Taken from the New International Version® (NIV), copyright © 1973, 1978, 1984, 2011 by Biblica, Inc. ®

to his purpose" (emphasis added). But how do we trust Jesus when we don't really know Him and when we don't know if we are "the called"? That is the beautiful part! For truly, the moment you choose to place your faith in Jesus Christ for salvation apart from any of your own effort or "good works," recognizing that you are sinful and in need of a Savior, His love will come rushing in like a tidal wave and will save you!

Salvation through the grace of Jesus Christ is the beginning point from which Jesus begins to turn all the pain and heartache around so that it is no longer defined by bitterness and shame but is repurposed into a testimony of triumph to help others. Our mistakes and brokenness can become a testimony of the goodness of God if we will give our pain to Jesus and ask Him to heal us. Titus 3:3–7 puts this transformation from sin to salvation into crystal-clear focus:

> For we ourselves also were sometimes foolish, disobedient, deceived, serving divers lusts and pleasures, living in malice and envy, hateful, and hating one another. But after that the kindness and love of God our Savior toward man appeared, not by works of righteousness which we have done, but according to his mercy he saved us, by the washing of regeneration, and renewing of the Holy Ghost; which he shed on us abundantly through Jesus Christ our Savior; that being justified by his grace, we should be made heirs according to the hope of eternal life.

Glory to God! Considering the banquet table of delights Jesus is offering, who would not want to partake? I think one of the greatest challenges of believing in the goodness of God comes from misinformation about Christianity and what it means to be a Christian. But if we set aside all preconceived ideas for a moment and just let the Word of God speak, it is possible to encounter the heart of God and be set free from the pain and sorrows of this world! After all, who wouldn't want that? The trouble is, the more abused, betrayed, and abandoned we've been, the less likely we are to believe that God cares at all about what happened to us, because the enemy will tempt us to believe that God is no longer good to us. But that is exactly what Lucifer—Satan, the prince of this world and enemy to God—*wants* you to believe! However, Jesus shows us a very different way—a much brighter future full of hope, prosperity, and joy—if only you will believe and ask Him to come to you and heal you.

There is a story of a woman in the Bible who chose to believe for a miracle from God even when she had suffered for many, many years with an "issue of blood" in her body; she was hemorrhaging. She had been sick for many years and had sought help from every physician she knew of, but no matter what the doctors tried to do, they couldn't heal her. Finally, she had spent so much money that she could no longer afford her doctors and had resigned herself to die. She had almost given up all hope. Then she heard of a certain prophet named Jesus who would be coming to her town. Even though she had very little strength left, she made her way out of her home and into the crowded streets of her town to try to meet Jesus. She may have hoped that He would pray for her or speak a blessing over her that could heal her, but instead she found herself on the ground and nearly being trampled by the crowd! Then the moment came when Jesus passed by, and in *faith* she reached out and barely touched the hem of the robe, or "garment," of Jesus and was healed in that very instant!

> And a woman having an issue of blood twelve years, which had spent all her living upon physicians, neither could be healed of any, came behind him, and touched the border of his garment: and immediately her issue of blood stanched [stopped]. And Jesus said, Who touched me? When all denied, Peter and they that were with him said, Master, the multitude [crowd] throng thee and press thee, and sayest thou, Who touched me? And Jesus said, Somebody hath touched me: for I perceive that virtue is gone out of me. And when the woman saw that she was not hid, she came trembling, and falling down before him, she declared unto him before all the people for what cause she had touched him, and how she was healed immediately. And he said unto her, Daughter, be of good comfort: thy faith hath made thee whole; go in peace. (Luke 8:43–48)

When the woman touched Jesus's robe, He felt virtue, or power, go out from Him (see Luke 8:46), and the woman was healed. I relate to this story because in a very real way, this is exactly what Jesus did for me, and He can do it for you, too! How did this happen? I was desperate and in need of healing in every way a person could need to be healed: physically, emotionally, mentally, and spiritually. At the time of my encounter with Jesus, I was literally in bed, sick and out of options. I had been ill for years with autoimmune diseases and was full of bitterness and unforgiveness. I needed deliverance and healing! In that state of total desperation and depravity, my hour of deliverance came. In a moment of crying out to God, I "reached for the hem of his garment." Jesus met me there and poured out His Spirit upon me, and I was supernaturally healed and made whole!

Interestingly, there is a cross-reference verse in my Bible tying Luke 8:43–48 to John 8:11, in which Jesus forgives the woman who was about to be stoned by a mob of angry men for committing adultery. Here we see in scripture how Jesus heals not only physically but also emotionally and spiritually. But notice what Jesus says to her regarding sin: "When Jesus had lifted up himself, and saw none but the woman, he said unto her, Woman, where are those thine accusers? hath no man condemned thee? She said, No man, Lord. And Jesus said unto her, Neither do I condemn thee: go, and sin no more" (John 8:10–11).

Now let us read the cross-references relating to this powerful passage of scripture about the power of forgiveness through a relationship with Jesus Christ:

> For God sent not his Son into the world to condemn the world; but that the world through him might be saved. (John 3:17)

> For the Son of man is not come to destroy men's lives, but to save them. (Luke 9:56)

> And he said unto him, Man, who made me a judge or a divider over you? (Luke 12:14)

Afterward Jesus findeth him in the temple, and said unto him, Behold, thou are made whole: sin no more, lest a worse thing come unto thee. (John 5:14)[15]

It is very important that we understand what Jesus is saying to us in scripture in the above passage with its accompanying cross-reference verses. When we cry out to Jesus with sincere, repentant, broken, and contrite hearts, He is faithful to forgive us of our sins and restore us. But He is giving us a warning as well to "go and sin no more." Jesus states that if we stay in rebellion and sin after being pardoned of that sin, or after being forgiven, we are putting ourselves at risk of a "worse thing" happening to us as a consequence of that sin. The point is not that God wants to punish you for sin. The warning is that the enemy, who is Satan, wants to ensnare you and keep you in bondage to sin. Therefore, it is extremely important that once we have been forgiven of sin, we do not return to it: "Then goeth he and taketh with himself seven other spirits more wicked than himself, and they enter in and dwell there: and the last state of that man is worse than the first. Even so shall it be also unto this wicked generation" (Matthew 12:45).

Remember that God's desire is to turn all things for our good, as Romans 8:28 states. Let's revisit these cross-references from 2 Timothy 1:9 that describe our true identity in Christ: "Who hath saved us, and called us with an holy calling, not according to our works, but according to his own purpose and grace, which was given us in Christ Jesus before the world began." And from 2 Timothy 1:9 we are led to Ephesians 1:4, which reads, "According as he hath chosen us in him before the foundation of the world, that we should be holy and without blame before him in love." And from here we are told we are God's elect: "Elect according to the foreknowledge of God the Father, through sanctification of the Spirit, unto obedience and sprinkling of blood of Jesus Christ: Grace unto you, and peace, be multiplied" (1 Peter 1:2). Finally, Romans 1:7 states, "beloved of God, called to be saints: Grace to you and peace from God our Father, and the Lord Jesus Christ."

---

[15]   See Mark 2:5: "When Jesus saw their faith, he said unto the sick of the palsy, Son, thy sins be forgiven thee."

What a rich heritage awaits those who place their faith and trust in Jesus! It won't always be easy, and the journey may get rough, but God's promise is sure: "I will never leave you nor forsake you" (Joshua 1:5 NIV; see also Deuteronomy 31:6 NIV). With man, this is impossible, but with God, *all things are possible* (Matthew 19:26).

But how do we trust someone we don't even *know*? That is the million-dollar question, isn't it? I thought I knew Jesus until the day He came to me in the crisis of my life—when my life itself was hanging in the balance—and changed me completely! I am a living testimony that knowing *about* Jesus is not the same as *knowing* Jesus.

If you are at a crossroads, wondering if God can be trusted, or if you've reached the point of no return and think you are beyond saving—friend, it's never too late to fall safely into the arms of Jesus! Or perhaps you've been a believer for year, but find your relationship with God to be stale and unsatisfying and you simply dread the monotony of life. Perhaps you are burdened by financial pressures and don't see a way out. Wherever you are on your journey, there is no judgment here. I simply want to encourage you to believe that Jesus is the answer to every problem known to humanity. It's my desire to witness to you that Jesus can make you whole! I have seen it over and over again in my own life and in the lives of others as I have witnessed men and women healed at our encounter retreats! It all starts with saying yes to Jesus!

Know this: Jesus is the deliverer who has come to set us free! His plans for you are good, now and forever, and He can be trusted! Ten years later, after my own deliverance and healing, I can honestly say that I have never been more joyful and at peace. Is life still hard sometimes? Sure it is! Have I ever struggled with fear or doubt? Of course I have! The difference is that those crippling emotions that used to shut me down no longer have that kind of power over me because I know who my God is and what He did for me on that rugged cross over two thousand years ago! And I know that I am who God says I am and not who others say I am!

What better friend could we have than Jesus, who was willing to literally lay down His life for His friends? That's my Jesus! He is the lover of my soul, my best friend, my comforter, and my protector—my "kinsman redeemer" (Leviticus 25:25; Ruth 3:2, 9; 4:8–10, 13–15). This is the Jesus I pray you will come to know! I pray with all my heart that you will choose today to take that leap of faith and simply ask Jesus to come and reveal Himself to you! If you are already a believer, I pray you will be empowered by the Holy Spirit to receive a fresh impartation to trust Jesus more and more! That is the power of a true relationship with Jesus Christ!

If you find yourself still unsure and asking the same million-dollar question I had burning in my mind ten years ago—"Can I trust you, God?"—then I pray that my story will help you find an ability to hope again, and to trust in a loving God who is full of mercy and grace and who has a good plan for your life, full of hope and a bright future!

Hope Shining Through the Dark

I will never forget feeling numb and empty and utterly lost years ago, during my divorce, while I was standing in a Cracker Barrel, a favorite family restaurant and gift shop. It was Christmastime—a time of year I normally loved—but that year, all my hopes and dreams were crashing down around me. My throat felt dry and parched, and my chest was tight and burning as my broken heart tried to accept the reality that life with my precious family and my darling children would never be the same. Soon I would be required to split time with my children from this Christmas forward, every other weekend. How could this happen to me? I felt angry, hopeless, bitter, used up, thrown away, and done.

"What was it all for?" was the cry of my heart. The sacrificing, the suffering, the hoping, and the praying for God to heal my broken marriage seemed to have been fruitless. While wandering the store, my eyes fell upon a plaque bearing a scripture from Jeremiah that I had never seen before: "'For I know the plans I have for you, declares the LORD, plans to prosper you and not to harm you, plans to give you hope and a future'" (Jeremiah 29:11 NIV).

My despair lifted with the thought that even in the midst of utter failure, God's plans for me could still be *good*. I felt the love of God flood my heart and mind in an unprecedented way as the tears welled up in my eyes. Something had changed in my heart. The light of hope had shined on me. What was the hope? It was the realization that God loved me and actually desired to help me through the mess I was in. Looking back, I can see that throughout my life, I knew who Jesus was, but I really didn't *know Him*. *Jesus is God* and He is full of grace, mercy, and love, and He died for sinners just like me! All at once, relief from the burden of perfection came with the realization that I was broken and needed a Savior more than ever.

I stood there stunned at the thought, daring myself to believe it could be true: that despite all my failures and brokenness and sin, Jesus might actually want to *help* me by giving me a hope and a future, even when my life was crumbling—*especially* when my life was crumbling, as a result of my sin and the sins of others. In my world, a "hope and a future" were the last things I would expect to receive while going through a divorce, because for me, I wasn't just getting divorced—I was experiencing a total crisis of faith, and I had no idea where that would take me.

It has been said that the definition of insanity is doing the same thing over and over again and expecting a different result. That day, I was ready to get off the insanity train! This scripture from Jeremiah delivered an unexpected shot of hope into my heart that God might actually have a *plan* for my life! I immediately purchased the scripture plaque, wrapped it, and placed it under the tree for myself so I could open it on Christmas morning and take in the truth of it again—the truth that God could actually love me and had a plan for me despite my flaws, failures, and faithlessness.

That Christmas morning, while opening my gift from Jesus, I wept tears of sweet assurance as the healing truth finally began to take root in my heart: *grace is a free gift of God* that is given when we least deserve it. Receiving the grace only Jesus can give rescued me from myself—broken, stubborn, rebellious me—unfolding a new plan, hope, and a future far better than anything I could have dreamed of! That Christmas morning, choosing hope and surrender unveiled the most beautiful gift of all: the freeing grace of Jesus Christ!

You Don't Have to Be Perfect!

I realize now that all those years living under a false religion of rule-keeping and ritual did not produce the dividends of an intimate relationship with the Lord, but rather an unhealthy, controlling relationship in which I lived in fear, wondering if God would stop loving me or punish me if I did not obey perfectly. I know now that God is so much more loving than that! His love is deeper and wider than we can imagine! Scripture says that the love of Jesus is so expansive that it can be compared to covering the whole earth: "As far as the east is from the west, so far hath he removed our transgressions from us" (Psalm 103:12).

It is truly humbling to take in the reality that Jesus loves us so much that He wants to forgive us—even when we are in rebellion and sin—and that He would choose to lay down His very own life as a final sacrifice, to shed His blood for mankind's sin, so that we could be forgiven of our sins. "For then must he often have suffered since the foundation of the world: but now once in the end of the world hath he appeared to put away sin by the sacrifice of himself" (Hebrews 9:26). Alternatively, the NASB 1995 reads, "Otherwise, He would have needed to suffer often since the foundation of the world; but now once at the consummation of the ages He has been manifested to put away sin by the sacrifice of Himself" (Hebrews 9:26). In the latter version, the word "consummation" is used to mean "the completion of the ages," or the completion of the plan for the salvation of mankind through the sacrifice of Jesus for our sins.

When I began to allow myself to imagine the possibility that God could love me even in the midst of deep failure, rebellion, and sin, my life began to change. Even though I had not fully encountered the love of Jesus, He was supernaturally drawing me to Him with His love, grace, and mercy. We must never underestimate the power of God's great grace to save the sinner! Jesus Himself said, "I came not to call the righteous, but sinners to repentance" (Luke 5:32). He called them to repentance that they could encounter the heart of God! Jesus spoke this intention directly to the Pharisees, who were murmuring and criticizing Jesus and His ministry because He dined with and focused His time on ministering to sinners and publicans, who were deeply despised by the Jewish religious leaders. Note Jesus's response to this criticism: "And Jesus answering said unto them, They that are whole need not a physician; but they that are sick. I came not to call the righteous, but sinners to repentance" (Luke 5:31–32). The NASB 1995 says it this way:

"And Jesus answered and said to them, 'It is not those who are well who need a physician, but those who are sick. I have not come to call the righteous but sinners to repentance'" (Luke 5:31–32). The Passion Translation (TPT) reads as follows:

> Matthew wanted to throw a banquet to honor Jesus. So he invited Jesus to his home for dinner, along with many of Levi's fellow tax collectors and other guests. But the Jewish religious leaders and experts of the law complained to Jesus' disciples, "Why would you defile yourselves by eating and drinking with tax collectors and sinners? *Doesn't Jesus know it's wrong to do that?*" Jesus overheard their complaining and said, "Who goes to the doctor for a cure? Those who are well or those who are sick? I have not come to call the 'righteous,' but to call those who know they are sinners and bring them to repentance." (Luke 5:29–32)

If you were to find yourself in the midst of total failure, unable to measure up to someone's expectations—whether it be your parents, your spouse, your church, or your community—what would motivate you to repent and change? Would public shaming, condemnation, and fear bring the desired result? Or would you rather have someone put an arm around you and say, "Look, I understand. I've been there. It's going to be okay. I will help you, because you are worthy of love and respect, and because I love you." Which approach would motivate you?

And it's not that Jesus is saying, "Hey, I only care about messed up, sinful people." Jesus loves all His children, but He knows that people who are already in a relationship with Him are abiding in Him and have come to understand how to access His love and grace. But the sinners who are lost in the darkness of the power of the enemy, who don't know where to begin or how to access Jesus through a personal relationship with Him—those are the ones Jesus can and will rescue— every time! Jesus loves all of us and wants everyone to come to Him and be saved. However, in Luke 5:31, Jesus reminds the religious Pharisees and Sadducees, those who considered themselves "righteous," that He has come not to call the righteous, but to call the sinners—those who are trapped in sin and in need of repentance. It is worth mentioning as well that the religious leaders did not consider themselves to be sinful at all, even though they were deep in spiritual pride. Yes, they knew the law of Moses and all the holy scriptures, but they considered themselves not really in *need* of saving or in need of a Savior. As a result, the religious leaders did not recognize Jesus as the Messiah!

Personally, I've lived on both sides of the fence. For the first thirty-eight years of my life, I considered myself "righteous" because of my religious upbringing. I was raised in the Mormon "church" and jumped through every possible religious hoop to prove myself and to win the approval of my parents, church leaders and peers. I went to seminary. I went to the "right" private, church-approved university. I married a man who met the criteria of a future "religious leader" in the approved wedding ceremony of my religious upbringing. I was a stay-at-home mom and poured everything I had into my children. If I was going to do something, I was going to do it to the best of my ability. I was an overachiever to say the least, but the funny thing is that I never felt good enough! I raised a special-needs child and volunteered at the school. I gave at least twenty hours per week of volunteer service at my church. I worked myself to the point of exhaustion! Then tragedy struck with the sudden passing of my beloved father and a deep betrayal from a close loved one, leaving me devastated and very wounded. My faith had been shaken. Because I did not understand the grace of God but was instead performance-driven and striving for perfection, I lived by the letter of the law rather than by grace and love.

Now, understand that if anyone had brought this to my attention at the time, I would have thought he or she was out of his or her mind! I considered myself to be very religious and a good person. But when push came to shove, I could not offer up something I did not have: *grace.* It wasn't until my life turned upside down during an unwanted divorce that I lost my bearings and didn't know what to believe in the wake of the devastation of betrayal and abandonment from every significant relationship I had. Suddenly all that "righteous living" wasn't holding up against the tidal wave of devastation that came crashing down over my life! In that place of facing my own failures and self-idolatry, I reacted to the circumstances of my life the way a lost person would, and I began to rebel. Why would I do that? Why would I rebel against God's laws if I was so "righteous"? I will tell you why: because I didn't have a clue about who Jesus really was and what He came for—*to save the sinner!* I was not aware of what it means to be in a blood-bought covenant relationship with Jesus through His sacrifice on the cross, in which He laid His own life down—for *me*. More than ever, I needed a revelation of Jesus and the power of encountering His love and grace so that I could enter into a surrendered relationship with Him and be free.

And then, like Paul, I encountered Jesus, and nothing was ever the same again. Glory to God! Jesus—*my Jesus*—stood beside me when no one else did! He rescued me in every way a person can be rescued. Truly, Jesus is our great and mighty defender:

> The LORD thy God the midst of thee is mighty; he will save, he will rejoice over thee with joy; he will rest in his love, he will joy over thee with singing. (Zephaniah 3:17)

Jesus healed me in every way a person needs to be healed, and He is daily singing over me with His love I believe with all my heart that Jesus desires to offer you a personal, intimate relationship with Him that has the power to fill every void and heal every hurt and loss. Jesus desires for you to truly know what it means to *know* Him and is ready to offer you a wonderful future full of hope, love, forgiveness, and joy. Will you receive it? Jesus is not only asking "Do you know me?" —He is asking you, "Do you *want* to know me?"

FOUR

He Heals Your Broken Heart

He healeth the broken in heart, and bindeth up their wounds.
—Psalm 147:3

J esus wants to heal your broken heart. He is aware of your suffering and all the losses, all the fear and pain. He is the "great physician" (Luke 5:31–32; Psalm 103:2–3), and He is able to "bind up," or put back together, the broken pieces of your heart. So many people today are living as the "walking wounded" and are broken in heart and spirit and need healing! The Hebrew word used in Psalm 147:3 for "broken" is "*shawbar*," which *Strong's Concordance* translates as "to break, break in or down, rend violently, wreck, crush, or quench." It can also mean "to be wrecked," and "to be broken or [figuratively] crushed" and "shattered."[16] I'm sure we can all relate to this feeling—the feeling of being *overcome* by grief and despair. I believe that at some point in each of our lives, each one of us will be there. Each one of us will reach his or her own "crucible" or "breaking point." How we get through that season of life and what follows has a lot to do with what we believe and *whom* we believe in. If we believe in God and trust that His plan for us is good, regardless of our life circumstances or what we see in the "natural realm," we will be able to keep a godly perspective as we experience hard things in life. Going further, if we believe in Jesus Christ and trust in His deity as a member of the threefold chord of God's

---

[16] James Strong, *Strong's Exhaustive Concordance of the Bible* (Nashville, Tennessee: Abingdon Press, 1986) H7665.

Holy Trinity—God the Father, Jesus the Son, and the Holy Spirit—we can access the strength we need to face any trial in life that comes, when we do as scripture says: "Submit yourselves therefore to God. Resist the devil, and he will flee from you" (James 4:7).

Jesus loves you, and He is waiting in the wings to heal your broken heart. He has suffered and experienced every infirmity, betrayal, heartache, and loss. No one can comfort us better than Jesus can! One of the most devastating experiences of my life was the result of betrayal from the people closest to me. When family boundaries are broken, when spiritual leaders fail, when spouses cheat or leave, or when children rebel, we can feel brokenhearted. So what do we do if we don't believe there is a God or that anyone truly cares about our problems, pain, and suffering? Many people are brokenhearted today and are facing horrendous challenges emotionally, physically, and financially, and they are turning to the world's solutions to solve their problems. But the truth is that no human being was created or designed to be able to handle the pain and turmoil of a broken heart. Eventually the weight of that brokenness will wear people out—both those who are trying to help and those who are carrying the burden. This is why the Word tells us, "[Cast] all your care upon him; for he careth for you" (1 Peter 5:7). Jesus also told us to come to Him, and that He would carry our burdens: "Come unto me, all ye that labour and are heavy laden, and I will give you rest. Take my yoke upon you, and learn of me; for I am meek and lowly in heart: and ye shall find rest unto your souls. For my yoke is easy, and my burden is light" (Matthew 11:28–30).

Jesus Himself has been there. In the Garden of Gethsemane, He faced the fear, pain, and agony of what was before Him; He suffered and agonized over the brokenness of the world and bore our grief, pain, and sorrow there; He willingly laid His life down for us by allowing Himself to be cruelly and brutally crucified upon a cross. Jesus obeyed the Father, suffered, bled, and died for our grief, sorrow, and pain so we could live! "But he was wounded for our transgressions, he was bruised for our iniquities [sins]: the chastisement of our peace was upon him; and with his stripes [lashings upon his back by a whip] we are healed" (Isaiah 53:5).

Jesus is fully able to comfort those who mourn, and He heals the brokenhearted!

Jesus Sacrificed Himself to Set You Free!

I want to testify to you today that we can truly place our faith and trust in Jesus Christ to heal us. He will comfort us in our trials and tribulations and bring healing to our broken hearts! We can choose to receive the love and grace of Jesus, entering into a relationship with Him, and finally *be free!* How is it done? It is done by His lovingkindness, compassion, grace, mercy, and power! Jesus is the God who saves! He is the Messiah, the Christ, the Anointed One who has come to save us from the sins of this world! As shared previously, in the midnight hour of my life, when I felt I could not survive what was happening in my life, that I could not endure, that I could not carry on because the weight of it all was just too much, I finally reached the end of myself and cried out to Jesus from the brokenness of my depleted heart. It was from this place of great desperation and need that I encountered Jesus and His love, healing my broken heart. Not only that, but Jesus put me in my right mind, restoring me back to the "first" and healing me of my all infirmities (emotional, mental, spiritual, and physical), and delivered me from demonic torment, condemnation, anxiety, shame, and fear. Truly, Jesus Christ delivered me in every way a person can be delivered!

At the time this happened, I did not know this deep level of healing was even possible. I wasn't even asking Jesus to heal me. I simply desired to hope that I might be able to comprehend the message of His grace, power, and love, and that somehow I could be forgiven for my own failings and "falling down." At that time in my life, I had been hearing the good news of Jesus Christ in a local Christian church but was struggling to truly receive it. I wanted to know whether this "good news" was really good news or just another disappointing religious lie. I had believed in a religious system that had failed me in every way, and I was not ready to jump right in and embrace "religion." I knew that I needed a miracle in my life, but I had no idea just how big of a miracle God was about to pour out over me!

Truly, Jesus heard the sincere cry of my broken heart and healed me! Psalm 51:17 tells us that the sacrifices of God are a broken and contrite heart. In the Old Testament law, which God gave to Moses for the instruction and protection of His people, the high priest would enter a special room in the tabernacle, or tent, in the wilderness where God's people were as they traveled on their way to the Promised Land God had prepared for them. Once a year, in the special room in the tabernacle called the "Holy of Holies," God would have the high priest sacrifice a lamb and then sprinkle the blood of the lamb onto the "mercy seat," which was the covering of the ark of the covenant, the resting place of God's presence. This ritual on the Day of Atonement symbolized that one day the blood of the Lamb, who is Jesus Christ, would be shed, or "poured out," for us, to heal us from our sins and infirmities, grief, and sorrows. (See Leviticus 16; Hebrews 9:1–14.)

When Jesus came to this world, He became a "man of sorrows" (Isaiah 53:3), enduring every kind of suffering a human being could experience in this life so that He could comfort us in our sorrows and understand what we are going through. Jesus kept His promise to us, enduring human suffering in every form and bleeding and dying on the cross so that we could be healed of our sorrows, pain, and sins.

Jesus was the final sacrifice, breaking the curse of sin. Likewise, God honors our "sacrifice" of a willing heart as we bring to Him our brokenness and allow Jesus to heal us, deliver us, and set us free! But there must be a spirit of cooperation involved: to be healed, we must first choose to allow Jesus to "come in" and heal us! Only then can we truly be free! He is so eager to heal you, to love you, and to minister to you in the midst of your brokenness: "Behold, I stand at the door, and knock: if any man hear my voice, and open the door, I will come in to him, and will sup [dine] with him, and he with me" (Revelation 3:20).[17]

Oh, if we only knew how much Jesus loves us! He is standing on the other side of the door of our heart, gently knocking, hoping we will soften our hearts, hear His voice, and let Him in! For this to truly happen, we must have hearts that have been humbled (or broken enough) to admit that we need help from God. At some point in our lives, we

---

[17]   See Luke 12:36–37: "And ye yourselves like unto men that wait for their lord, when he will return from the wedding; that when he cometh and knocketh, they may open unto him immediately. Blessed *are* those servants, whom the lord when he cometh shall find watching: verily I say unto you, that he shall gird himself, and make them to sit down to meat, and will come forth and serve them."

have to reach a point of knowing that we can't make it on our own. This is what I like to call "reaching the end of ourselves." This heart condition is highlighted in Isaiah 57:15: "I dwell in the high and holy place, with him also that is of a contrite and humble spirit, to revive the spirit of the humble, and to revive the heart of the contrite ones."

According to *Strong's Concordance*, the Hebrew word "contrite" means crushed.[18] Can we just pause and take in the beauty and power of this verse? Jesus is saying to you and me that to be crushed in the spirit, or to have a broken heart, is to be in a "holy place." Why is it holy? It is holy because in this place of intense crushing of the heart—brokenness, unfulfilled dreams, unmet expectations, loss, despair, fear, anxiety, and pain—*you can meet the heart of Jesus*, who is holy, righteous, faithful, true, and more than able to put your broken heart back together! This is *how* we reach the level of humility Jesus is searching for! Let's look at the definition of the word "humble" in *Webster's New Dictionary, 1st edition*: "having or showing a consciousness of one's shortcomings; modest; lowly; unpretentious."[19] In other words, we no longer think too highly of ourselves but instead are willing to admit our own depravity before God and ask for help! Now let's look at the *Strong's Concordance* definition of the Hebrew word "to humble": "To trample, prostrate, humble self, submit self."[20]

To be prostrate before the Lord means to be bowed low with one's face on the ground. This is a powerful visual example of humility! Pride will keep the door to our hearts barred shut with Jesus standing on the other side. Humility is a key that will unlock the door, allowing Jesus to come into your heart and set you free!

The Woman Who Loved Much

As I mentioned earlier, there was a woman who was very close to Jesus during His ministry. She was not a holy, righteous, clean,

---

[18]   Strong, H1792, H1793.

[19]   Webster's New Dictionary, 1st ed. Michael Agnes. (Cleveland, OH: Wiley Publishing, Inc. 2003), s.v. "Humble."

[20]   Strong, H7511.

well-respected, and admired woman. Rather, she had seven demons and was likely living the life of a prostitute. I think it is reasonable to believe that under those life circumstances, this woman was crushed, broken, and afraid. But one day, Jesus crossed her path, and her life was never the same! Scripture doesn't say how they met, but we know that the impact of her meeting Him changed her to the core—so much so that she was willing to break through all religious protocols and force her way into a room of self-righteous Pharisees while they were dining with Jesus! Then she did the unthinkable. She threw herself at the feet of Jesus, prostrate before Him, and humbly, with a crushed, broken heart, began to wash His feet with her hair and her tears and to anoint His feet with oil. Jesus was so moved by her love that He in that very moment used her love as a witness to show the Pharisees what real saving faith looked like. Naturally, the Pharisees responded with great disdain and strongly objected to a filthy prostitute entering their living quarters and interrupting their dinner. In other words, they were *proud.* But Jesus shocked them all with His declaration that her sins were forgiven because she loved Jesus much. She honored Him and placed her faith in His deity. From this act of love and faith, Jesus declared to this woman that her faith had *saved her* "Wherefore I say unto thee, Her sins, which are many, are forgiven; for she loved much: but to whom little is forgiven, the same loveth little" (Luke 7:47).

What a stunning picture of the grace and love of Jesus this story portrays! The cross-references in my Bible highlight even further the goodness of His love for the sinner who repents:

> And the grace of our Lord was exceeding abundant with
> faith and love which is in Christ Jesus. (1 Timothy 1:14)[21]

---

[21] See 1 Corinthians 3:10: "According to the grace of God which is given unto me, as a wise masterbuilder, I have laid the foundation, and another buildeth thereon. But let every man take heed how he buildeth thereupon." See also Titus 2:2: "That the aged men be sober, grave [reverent], temperate, sound in faith, in charity, in patience."

Moreover the law entered, that the offence might abound. But where sin abounded, grace did much more abound. (Romans 5:20)[22]

And they that sat at meat with him began to say within themselves, Who is this that forgiveth sins also? (Luke 7:49)[23]

And he said to the woman, Thy faith hath saved thee; go in peace. (Luke 7:50)[24]

Here in Scripture, we see Jesus demonstrating through comparison the difference between pride and humility: the Pharisees (proud religious believers) are contrasted with the sinners who come to Jesus in repentance and humility (those with crushed and contrite hearts). Humility is what Jesus is looking for! This is the sacrifice the Lord will seek and will honor!

The sacrifices of God are a broken spirit: a broken and a contrite heart, O God, thou wilt not despise. (Psalm 51:17)

The LORD is nigh unto them that are of a broken heart; and saveth such as be of a contrite spirit. (Psalm 34:18)

He healeth the broken in heart, and bindeth up their wounds. He telleth the number of the stars; he calleth

---

22   See John 15:22: "If I had not come and spoken unto them, they had not had sin: but now they have no cloke [excuse] for their sin."

23   See Matthew 9:3: "And, behold, certain of the scribes said within themselves, This *man* blasphemeth." See also Mark 2:7: "Why doth this *man* thus speak blasphemies? who can forgive sins but God only?"

24   See Matthew 9:22: "But Jesus turned him about, and when he saw her, he said, Daughter, be of good comfort; thy faith hath made thee whole. And the woman was made whole from that hour." See also Mark 5:34: "And he said unto her, Daughter, thy faith hath made thee whole; go in peace, and be whole of thy plague." See also Mark 10:52: "And Jesus said unto him, Go thy way; thy faith hath made thee whole. And immediately he received his sight, and followed Jesus in the way."

them all by their names. Great is our Lord, and of great power: his understanding is infinite. ⁶The LORD lifteth up the meek: he casteth the wicked down to the ground. Sing unto the LORD with thanksgiving; sing praise upon the harp unto our God … The LORD taketh pleasure in them that fear [are in awe of] him, in those that hope in his mercy. (Psalm 147:3–7, 11)

Now let's continue on with the passage from Luke 7 and "lean in close" with our spirits to hear and receive the *life-changing* words Jesus spoke to this woman of faith as she so beautifully demonstrated her love for Him:

- Can we receive the words Jesus said to the sinful woman and the underlying principles for ourselves today?
- "Your many sins are forgiven because of your great love for Me."
- We love big when we know how much we have been forgiven.
- We love little when we have not experienced Jesus's forgiveness of our sins.
- The Pharisees chose legalism and judgment of Jesus's bold statement, saying, "Who is this who forgives sins also?"
- Jesus makes one of the most profound statements in the *entire Bible!* He tells the woman her *faith* has saved her.
- "Go in peace."

It is my most sincere prayer that we will choose to receive the words Jesus spoke to the sinful woman for ourselves today. What about you? Does it feel hard to believe that we could be forgiven of great sin simply because we choose to believe by faith in Jesus Christ? Well, that is exactly what happened here in Scripture! In fact, while this woman was anointing the feet of Jesus, He shared a parable, or story, with the Pharisees to demonstrate the magnitude of what was happening right before their very eyes!

There was a certain creditor which had two debtors: the one owed five hundred pence, and the other fifty.[25] And when they had nothing to pay, he frankly forgave them both. Tell me therefore, which of them will love him most? Simon answered and said, I suppose that he, to whom he forgave most. And he said unto him, Thou hast rightly judged. (Luke 7:41–43)

I believe with my whole heart that Jesus does not want to hold our sins against us but deeply desires to see us forgiven and set free! All Jesus is asking for is a pure sacrifice of a broken and contrite heart, and a desire to repent of our sin. He wants us to know that no matter what we have done, no matter how bad the sin, He is ready and willing to forgive us and set us free. Jesus understands that the greater the sin, the greater the deliverance and freedom that will come to us once we allow Him to speak life, healing, and forgiveness over our brokenness! The greater the debt we have incurred with sin, the greater the gratitude we will have when the debt is removed. No amount of effort or proving our faithful obedience will suffice, because no human being is capable of living a perfect life or of following God's laws to the letter. That is where the phrase "letter of the law" comes from. It implies exactness and perfection, which no human being is capable of. Why not? Because we will never be that perfect! We all fall down sometimes! We all need Jesus! The truth is, we cannot make it to heaven without Him! Remember, Jesus loves you and is waiting and ready to heal your broken heart, if you will let Him.

Would you like to experience this freedom and healing from the forgiveness of Jesus?

Pray this prayer with me:

---

[25] See Matthew 18:28: "But the same servant went out, and found one of his fellowservants, which owed him an hundred pence: and he laid hands on him, and took *him* by the throat, saying, Pay me that thou owest." See also Mark 6:37: "He answered and said unto them, Give ye them to eat. And they say unto him, Shall we go and buy two hundred pennyworth of bread, and give them to eat?"

Lord Jesus, I know I have sinned. The hurts of this world and the hurt I have caused myself and others is too much to bear. Lord Jesus, I invite you to come and meet me here. Please bind up my broken heart, heal me of all offenses and wrongs, and lead me in your love and forgiveness. I love you, Lord. In Jesus' name, Amen!

FIVE

The Potter

But now, O Lord, thou art our father; we are the clay, and
thou our potter; and we all are the work of thy hand.
—Isaiah 64:8

When you look in the mirror, what do you see? This is something I struggled with for the majority of my life, because looking in the mirror while dressing for the day always brought the painful reminder of a physical deformity that made me feel as though I was "damaged goods," "ugly," and "undesirable." Now, before you go thinking that I am out of my mind, let me share with you the old adage "You can't judge a book by its cover." What I mean by that is this: on the outside, I may have been pleasant-looking, but under the surface there was a huge secret that was eating a hole into my soul. But after I was touched by the love of Jesus, that all changed.

The truth is that no one is perfect. Every one of us has been and again will be a broken vessel that Jesus lovingly restores with His grace, mercy, and power—and this is what we were destined for from before the foundation of the world: to be changed from vessels prepared for wrath to vessels of mercy through the grace of Jesus and the power of the Holy Spirit! Heaven knows we need the healing of Jesus! I want to share my heart with you now about our true identity in Jesus Christ, because once we understand who we truly are in the Lord, everything changes!

For thou hast possessed my reins: thou hast covered me in my mother's womb. I will praise thee; for I am fearfully and wonderfully made: marvelous are thy works; and that my soul knoweth right well. My substance was not hid from thee, when I was made in secret, and curiously wrought in the lowest parts of the earth. Thine eyes did see my substance, yet being unperfect [unformed]; and in thy book all my members were written, which in continuance were fashioned, when as yet there was none of them. How precious also are thy thoughts unto me, O God! how great is the sum of them! (Psalm 139:13–17)

I really want you to hear me loud and clear: Our brokenness is beautiful to Jesus because He was broken for you so that the broken pieces of your life could be put back together through His love, grace, and mercy. Hallelujah!

The Lord is so personal and knows us intimately; even from our mother's womb, He foreknew us! It's almost too much to take in. It's not for us to ask the Potter why He formed the clay into the vessel that we now are (Isaiah 45:9), but it is up to us to surrender to His will, asking, "Lord, what would You have me do with how You've made me, with what You've created me to be? How can I best shine light into darkness with the life You've given me?" The reality is that some people are missing limbs or are overweight or too skinny or have acne or illness. Still other people struggle with pains that are never seen with the natural eye: those who are emotionally, sexually, verbally, or spiritually abused and tormented.

When I began ministry, I studied through a manual written to help ministry leaders identify women who are being abused. I will never forget the moment my brain began to process that I had personally suffered from four of the five ways a woman can experience abuse in relationships! I wept and wept, and then I had a moment of realization: *God has allowed me to have these experiences! There must be a reason!* The reason that I have come to embrace is that "life happens" and that what counts is what I do with what I have been given, not what I have lost! I truly believe that nothing is a mistake. Everything occurs on purpose for a purpose. Even the pain, the sorrow, the loss, and the heartache serve a purpose, for it is when life becomes blackest black that we know the light is about to dawn! The truth is that the Lord has never abandoned me. He has faithfully been with me from the foundation of the world, because that is what scripture tells me about my true identity in Christ:

> Blessed be the God and Father of our Lord Jesus Christ, who hath blessed us with all spiritual blessings in heavenly places in Christ: according as he hath chosen us in him before the foundation of the world, that we should be holy and without blame before him in love: having predestinated us unto the adoption of children by Jesus Christ to himself, according to the good pleasure of his will, to the praise of the glory of his grace, wherein he hath made us accepted in the beloved. In whom we have redemption through his blood, the forgiveness of sins, according to the riches of his grace. (Ephesians 1:3–7)

I am chosen from the foundation of the world to burn with passion for Jesus! I am holy and without blame. I am predestined to become adopted by Jesus Christ Himself. I am accepted. I have redemption by His blood. I am forgiven of my sins because of the riches of *His grace*.

It's almost too beautiful to believe, isn't it? I can hear you saying, "But you don't know *my story*." Friend, if it's feeling next to impossible for you to believe God could be this good, let me share with you some of my true story, not to compare notes or one-up anyone, but to be authentic and real. No one wants to be lied to. From my story, I believe that you will see the love, grace, mercy, and power of Jesus shining through the darkest, blackest moments of my life, because that is when God is most glorified!

I was born with a rare condition that caused a physical deformity, which led to feelings of insecurity about my physical appearance. In my elementary school years, some classmates found out about my condition and bullied me daily for several years. This was an extremely painful experience that caused me to carry emotional wounds and feelings of rejection.

By age twelve, I underwent my first of ten painful surgeries to try to address the issue. I remember this being very difficult, painful, traumatizing, and frightening. I can still vividly remember the night of my first surgery. While lying in a hospital bed, my thoughts turned to a song by Amy Grant, a popular Christian artist, that I had recently heard on the radio. I remember being mesmerized hearing the names of God the first time I heard the song "El Shaddai." I began to sing that same song out loud from my hospital bed and felt the presence of Jesus all around me! I remember asking the young girl in the bed next to mine if she believed in Jesus. She said she did, and together, we sang to one another until we fell asleep. Looking back, the remarkable thing to me is that even though I had not prayed a "saving prayer," Jesus came to me in that moment and poured out His peace and love over my young, tender heart. At that time in my life, I had not even attended a Christian church, but the love of Jesus still met me there in the moment when my heart cried out to Him. How do I explain that? How is it done? The answer is found in scripture, which beautifully defines our true identity in Christ from before the foundation of the world (Ephesians 1:3–6).

Are you beginning to see the glory of our King Jesus shining through? Regardless of what we have been through in this life, if we have Jesus Christ as our Lord and Savior, there is truly nothing that we lack, and we are richly blessed! The Lord, in His divine wisdom and love, uses the hardships in our lives to draw us to Him so that we will be humbled. He softens our hearts to the point that we will finally cry out to Him in sincerity. This is surely how the Lord drew me out of the spiritual abuse of cult religion into His grace, mercy, and power. But I didn't get there on my own! It was the suffering that brought me to the blackest black, where the light of God's love could finally pierce the darkness of my wounded soul and deliver me straight into the arms of Jesus! It was a long thirty-eight-year wait, but finally the moment came when the love, grace, and mercy of Jesus Christ poured out over me, and He filled me up to overflowing with His grace and with the Holy Spirit! It was a supernatural deliverance for sure, and a testimony of just how good the mercy of God truly can be.

So what about you? Are there times in your life when you have wondered, "What was that all about, God? Why did I have to suffer like that?" When we come to understand that our Father is the Potter and we are the clay, we realize that He is the one who is shaping us, molding and forming us one step at a time, one process at a time. God will at times *allow* a "crushing" to occur that will transform us from what we were into something greater. I have come to understand that it is in the crushing, pressing, shaping, and reforming that our lives can be transformed into something entirely new and beautiful to give God glory! Try to imagine a lump of clay on the potter's wheel. It starts out looking just like a sticky, dull blob with no shape or form. Then, as the potter begins to turn the wheel and handle the clay again and again, that lump of clay begins to take a new shape and form. During this process, if the clay becomes flawed or damaged, the potter will do something drastic; he or she will smash down the vessel so it can be changed, reshaped, and formed into a new vessel of glory. Friends, do you see the connection?

When we begin to see the process God is taking each of us through in life—that we are truly on a journey, and we can be set free from regret, torment, and fear—then we can step into full trust and surrender as we allow God to mold us into vessels of mercy for His glory! "What if God, willing to shew his wrath, and to make his power known, endured with much longsuffering the vessels of wrath fitted to destruction: And that he might make known the riches of his glory on the vessels of mercy, which he had afore [before] prepared unto glory" (Romans 9:22–23).

I believe that so many testimonies will begin to flow out of our lives as we begin to see that God's plans for us are always good. When we cooperate with the will of God, the end result will always be better than the beginning. Scripture says it this way:

> For I know the thoughts that I think toward you, says the LORD, thoughts of peace and not of evil, to give you a future and a hope. (Jeremiah 29:11, NKJV)

> The glory of this latter house shall be greater than of
> the former, saith the LORD of hosts: and in this place
> will I give peace, saith the LORD of hosts. (Haggai 2:9)

Each of us is, in a sense, "on the potter's wheel." Each of us is being changed from a vessel of wrath (once without the glory of God in us) to a beautiful, powerful vessel of mercy, formed, shaped, and cured in the fire for the glory of God! When we realize that God doesn't make mistakes and that His plans for us are always good, we begin to see the power of allowing ourselves to submit to the *process* of becoming who God has always intended for each of us to be.

Each one of us has his or her own story to tell. The Word says that we overcome the enemy by the blood of the Lamb and the word of our testimony (Revelation 12:11). I pray that we all will choose to step into the freedom that comes from embracing the truth that if you have accepted Jesus Christ as your Lord and Savior by faith and are walking in a personal relationship with Him, then you have already reached the point of victory by the blood of Jesus! If you have accepted Jesus, you are an overcomer and no longer need to be subject to the torment of spirits that follow Satan, for you are a blood-bought believer, protected by the blood of Jesus Christ through the power of the Holy Spirit! This is a powerful place to be, because when you know your true identity in Christ, you suddenly become the enemy's worst nightmare. You have the power to obliterate the darkness with the light of Christ and the Holy Spirit, who now resides inside of you and has the power to crush the enemy's lies, tricks, and torments. Just like that, your days of worry, fear, anxiety, torment, shame, condemnation, and illness can be over!

This is what truly happened to me after I encountered the love and grace of Jesus Christ! I was filled to overflowing with the grace, love, mercy, and power of Yeshua, the *God who saves*. This is how we become vessels of mercy for *His glory*. When we reach the place of brokenness and feel shattered like a clay potthat is where the Lord can step in and reform us, like clay on a potter's wheel, to become vessels restored by the mercy of God, fully cured by the fire of a furnace of trials. We will be transformed into beautiful, powerful, strong vessels of mercy so we can hold the glory of God inside of us and pour out the love of Jesus onto other broken people who need to know Him!

New Wine

We see the analogy of "new wine" being poured into us in Mark 2:18–22. Once we become a transformed vessel of mercy, we are able to hold the new wine of God's Holy Spirit inside the vessel—which is us! But to hold this "new wine," we must first be molded, shaped, formed, and cured by the Potter. Jesus explained that we cannot pour new wine into old wineskins because the old wineskins will burst: "And no man putteth new wine into old bottles: else the new wine doth burst the bottles, and the wine is spilled, and the bottles will be marred: but new wine must be put into new bottles" (Mark 2:22).

It is the same with us holding the Holy Spirit in our bodies. The Father, who is one with Jesus and the Holy Spirit, is the Potter who is molding us on the potter's wheel into vessels of mercy for His glory so that we can pour out His pure anointing that He has poured into us. We cannot be "glory carriers" of God's pure anointing and power unless we have been tested in the fiery furnace of trials and tribulations and withstood the heat! Only at this point in our spiritual lives will we become new, fresh wineskins that are strong and able to hold the new wine without bursting. When we become vessels of mercy for God's glory, we have been filled up to overflowing with the new wine of the Holy Spirit and will live in the overflow of love and the fruit of the Spirit (Galatians 5:22–23). To become a glory carrier of God's power, we must be sanctified by the love, grace, mercy, and power of Jesus Christ and filled up to overflowing with impartations of glory from the Holy Spirit.

The Prophetic Vision: Vessels of Mercy

We have established that God is a good God who loves you and wants good for you, and that faith and trust are keys that unlock the door to receiving His supernatural grace and mercy. In the summer of 2017, on the back deck of my cabin, while sitting in the sunlight after running our

Freedom in Christ retreat, I was spending time with Jesus, reading Romans 9.[26] As I was reading, I heard the Holy Spirit speak over me: "Look deeper. Read the verse about vessels of mercy again." So I went back and read it again, as well as every cross-reference, which, to my amazement, began to unfold some of the richest teachings I have ever read about the power of God to set us free and transform us into vessels of mercy for His glory!

Later that same day, while driving my car to a graduation ceremony where I would speak to women recovering from addiction, abuse, and homelessness, God gave me a vision that changed my life. Just hours later, I shared this vision with the women at the graduation. I experienced the anointing of God so powerfully that my whole body was trembling as I obeyed the Lord and told them what the He had shown me earlier that day. I pray you will receive this account of the mercy of our God fully into your heart, mind, and spirit.

While I was praising and worshipping, listening to a favorite worship song—"Forever" by Kari Jobe—I received revelation knowledge with images, or a vision in the Spirit. I saw images appearing as if I were watching a movie while my eyes were wide open, and by the power of the Holy Spirit, my mind and heart comprehended the meaning of the images simultaneously.

The vision began with an image of a tall, faded, and weathered clay wine pot, which was wider at the bottom and narrower toward the top. From the top of the clay pot, I saw red liquid bubbling up and out, gently flowing like a fountain, rolling down and over, covering every part of the clay pot. Then I heard words within my spirit: *"This is the blood of Jesus that cleanses every part of you."*

Next I saw a long and jagged crack down the front of the pot with light shining out of it, and I heard, *"My light shines through your brokenness."*

While receiving this vision, I asked, "Where is this pot, Lord?" The next image I received showed that the pot was sitting on the stone slab inside the burial tomb of Jesus! My eyes were then fixed on the white linen cloths that were under the pot and strewn over the slab. (White

---

[26]   To learn more about Be Free Ministry retreats, visit www.BeFreeInChrist Ministry.org.

linen is a symbol of righteousness, and we will all be wearing white at the throne, worshipping God in heaven; see Revelation 19:8.)

I then comprehended in the Spirit that I was gazing upon the linen burial clothes of the Messiah, King Jesus! I looked to the left, and I realized I was standing inside the garden tomb, and the light of God's glory was pouring in through an opening to my right, where I saw the azure-blue sky, which represented heaven, and puffy white clouds, which symbolized the glory of God (Exodus 40:34).

The final word I heard the voice of God speak was this:

"Broken vessels, changed into vessels of mercy for My glory."

God, knowing our sins would bring spiritual death, sent his Son, Jesus Christ, to die for our sins on the cross, redeeming us and setting us free from eternal damnation. Why would God allow this kind of audacious, radical mercy to fall on sinners? As scripture states, He does so to "make known the riches of *His glory*" (Romans 9:23). Why would God make such allowance of grace for sinners? Because God loves us and wants us to fulfill His calls on our lives that He has ordained for us from before the foundation of the world: "According as he hath chosen us in him before the foundation of the world, that we should be holy and without blame before him in love …" (Ephesians 1:4).[27]

The love and grace and power of Jesus to save a lost soul is stunning! I will *never* get over what Jesus has done for me! Truly, He rescued my lost soul from wrath and made me royalty. He removed my soiled clothing and gave me a white robe and gave me His "signet ring" with His seal and crest stamped upon it (Zechariah 3:4; Luke 15:22). He anointed my head with His oil of joy and placed a "royal diadem"—a golden crown—upon my head (Isaiah 61:3; Zechariah 3:5). This is *King Jesus*. He comes to rescue the fallen, the lost, the broken, the rejected and dejected, the abandoned ones, and He calls to us in the midst of our stormy seas of life, saying, "Call unto me, and I will answer thee, and

---

[27] See Romans 8:28: "And we know that all things work together for good to them that love God, to them who are the called according to *his* purpose." See also 1 Peter 1:2: "Elect according to the foreknowledge of God the Father, through sanctification of the Spirit, unto obedience and sprinkling of the blood of Jesus Christ: Grace unto you, and peace, be multiplied."

[show] thee great and mighty things, which thou knowest not" (Jeremiah 33:3).

"Instrument of Mine"

Our ultimate destiny is to become all God has created us to be and to use our giftings and anointing to bring Him glory! "But the Lord said to him, "Go, for he is a chosen instrument of Mine, to bear My name before the Gentiles and kings and the sons of Israel" (Acts 9:15, NASB 1995).

If you have been a recipient of the miracle of saving grace and filled to overflow with the power of the Holy Spirit by faith, then you have been changed into a vessel of His mercy for God's glory. You are now set apart, called, and chosen. Truly God is faithful! "Moreover whom he did predestinate, them he also called: and whom he called, them he also justified: and whom he justified, them he also glorified" (Romans 8:30).

Friend, I pray that your heart fully takes in the awesome miracle of grace, trusting that Jesus Christ has chosen to transform you from your broken, fallen state—from a "broken vessel"—into a vessel of *His mercy!*

SIX

The Faith of Abraham

And [Abraham] believed in the LORD; and he
counted it to him for righteousness.[28]
—Genesis 15:6

We see clearly throughout scripture that God has been consistent in keeping covenant throughout all time, starting with Abraham, the "father of faith," because it was through Abraham that God established His covenant of salvation by grace through faith with His people! Abraham believed God by faith when God told him that he would be the father of many nations. This seemed impossible because Abraham and his wife Sarah were old, and Sarah was past childbearing years. But Abraham chose to believe God's promises to him by faith, and scripture says that God credited it to him as righteousness (Genesis 15:6). Scripture tells us that we, as believers, are justified by faith when we choose to believe God by faith (Romans 3:27–28). Glory to God! It was not Abraham's good works that positioned him before God to be justified, but his choice to *believe* God. This choice to believe is also called the "hearing of faith":

---

28   See Genesis 21:1: "And the LORD visited Sarah as he had said, and the LORD did unto Sarah as he had spoken." See also Romans 4:3, 9, 22: "For what saith the scripture? Abraham believed God, and it was counted unto him for righteousness ... *Cometh* this blessedness then upon the circumcision *only*, or upon the uncircumcision also? for we say that faith was reckoned to Abraham for righteousness ... And therefore it was imputed to him for righteousness."

For if Abraham were justified by works, he hath whereof to glory [he would have had something to boast about]; but not before God. (Romans 4:2)

Therefore by the deeds of the law there shall no flesh be justified in his sight: for by the law is the knowledge of sin. (Romans 3:20)[29]

Where is boasting then? It is excluded. By what law? of works? Nay: but by the law of faith. (Romans 3:27)[30]

For what saith the scripture? Abraham believed God, and it was counted unto him for righteousness. (Romans 4:3)[31]

Here it is, as clear as day in scripture: we are justified, or declared righteous, before God unto salvation by placing our faith in Jesus Christ and receiving the Holy Spirit, which occurs by faith! If we think we should be declared righteous because of our "holiness" or because of our good works before God, we are simply operating in pride and boasting in our own efforts. We know and have seen in scripture that no one is made righteous by works, but only by placing faith in Jesus Christ as our Lord and Savior. If you equate your righteousness with your works or how well you are living your life, you will set yourself up for failure, stress, fear, and condemnation. In other words, you are creating an expectation for yourself that simply can't be met. This is how legalistic believers become taskmasters of themselves and others: they fall into the trap of performance-minded Christianity rather than *resting* in the grace of Jesus. When we place our faith in Jesus for

---

[29] See Psalm 143:2: "And enter not into judgment with thy servant: for in thy sight shall no man living be justified."

[30] See Romans 2:17: "Behold, thou art called a Jew, and restest in the law, and makest thy boast of God."

[31] See Genesis 15:6: "And he believed in the LORD; and he counted it to him for righteousness." See also Galatians 3:6: "Even as Abraham believed God, and it was accounted to him for righteousness." See also James 2:23: "And the scripture was fulfilled which saith, Abraham believed God, and it was imputed unto him for righteousness: and he was called the Friend of God."

salvation, we are safe in His care; He is faithful and will keep His word to us. The good news is that even when we are unfaithful, we can repent of our sins and return to Him (See 2 Timothy 2:13)! "God is not a man, that he should lie; neither the son of man, that he should repent: hath he said, and shall he not do it? or hath he spoken, and shall he not make it good?" (Numbers 23:19). God does not change His mind, and there is no variation in His Word. He will not take away the free gift of salvation that you believed for by faith, because God knows your heart and whether or not your confession of faith was sincere. God will not change, and He will not lie! "Every good gift and every perfect gift is from above, and cometh down from the Father of lights, with whom is no variableness, neither shadow of turning" (James 1:17).

When we believe this truth of God's unchanging character and His faithfulness to us, we finally begin to rest in the peace of Christ that passes all understanding, the peace that has the power to guard our hearts and minds in Christ Jesus (Philippians 4:7). His peace, love, and grace cover and surround your heart and mind with His truth and promises, that He will never leave you or forsake you! When we reach this level of faith, we can finally rest as we choose to trust Jesus:

> Blessed be the LORD, that hath given rest unto his people Israel, according to all that he promised: there hath not failed one word of all his good promise, which he promised by the hand of Moses his servant. (1 Kings 8:56)[32]

> Come unto me, all ye that labour and are heavy laden, and I will give you rest. Take my yoke upon you, and learn of me; for I am meek and lowly in heart: and ye shall find rest unto your souls. For my yoke is easy, and my burden is light. (Matthew 11:28–30)

It was never God's intention for us to carry an unnecessary burden or weight upon our shoulders alone—this is why He sent Jesus to redeem

---

[32]　See 1 Chronicles 22:18: "*Is* not the LORD your God with you? and hath he *not* given you rest on every side? for he hath given the inhabitants of the land into mine hand; and the land is subdued before the LORD, and before his people."

us and the Holy Spirit to comfort and heal our hearts with God's love! God loves us and wants us to have joy in Him. When sin entered the world, God provided His Son, Jesus Christ, to die for us so we could be free from the crushing weight of sin and be free from striving, fear, shame, unbelief, condemnation, and self-reliance. Allow the scripture to speak for itself, and receive the invitation to enter the "believer's rest":

> Let us therefore fear, lest, a promise being left us of entering into his rest, any of you should seem to come short of it.[33] For unto us was the gospel preached, as well as unto them: but the word preached did not profit them, not being mixed with faith in them that heard it. For we which have believed do enter into rest, as he said, As I have sworn in my wrath, if they shall enter into my rest: although the works were finished from the foundation of the world.[34] For he spake in a certain place of the seventh day on this wise, And God did rest the seventh day from all his works. And in this place again, If they shall enter into my rest. Seeing therefore it remaineth that some must enter therein, and they to whom it was first preached entered not in because of unbelief [disobedience]. (Hebrews 4:1–6)

And we see again that scripture is consistent with itself in these additional verses about faith and righteousness:

> Cometh this blessedness upon the circumcision only, or upon the uncircumcision also? for we say that faith was reckoned [imputed] to Abraham for righteousness. (Romans 4:9)

> And therefore it was imputed to [Abraham] for righteousness. (Romans 4:22)

---

[33] See 2 Corinthians 6:1: "We then, *as* workers together *with him*, beseech *you* also that ye receive not the grace of God in vain."

[34] See Psalm 95:11: "Unto whom I sware in my wrath that they should not enter into my rest."

> Even as Abraham believed God, and it was accounted to him for righteousness. (Galatians 3:6)

> And the scripture was fulfilled which saith, Abraham believed God, and it was imputed unto him for righteousness: and he was called the Friend of God. (James 2:23)

How precious is that? God calls us "righteous" and "justified" and His own *friend* by our choice to believe in Jesus Christ by faith! Hallelujah! Truly, those who enter this spiritual rest of trust and faith are the ones Jesus will call His friends.

Let's think on that for a moment, shall we? Imagine you are walking the beach with your very best friend, who then shares with you something very personal and dear to their heart. They ask you, with a huge smile on their face and eyes twinkling, "Do you believe me?" And your eyes fall to the sand, and you say, with a heavy heart, "No, I do not." This is what unbelief looks like to Jesus! He is waiting with great anticipation and joy to give you the greatest gift anyone could ever receive: *the gift of eternal life.* All we have to do is receive the gift and *believe.*

What we must understand is this: we can trust Jesus with our lives and believe that He will keep His promises to us because He is faithful and He proved His faithfulness with the shedding of His own blood on the cross to pay the price for our sins. Jesus is faithful even when we are not faithful (2 Timothy 2:13)! Truly, if we will choose to believe Jesus, admit our unbelief, repent of our sins, and ask Him to come be the Lord of our lives, we can receive the gift of eternal life! This decision will require you to make some personal changes and to repent from sin. But when the acceptance, love, grace, mercy, power, and joy of Jesus enter your heart, you will be empowered by Jesus Himself to face every area of sin and rebellion and defeat it. When you become one with Jesus by faith (John 17:21), you will have His blood and His power flowing through your veins to equip you with every good spiritual gift from heaven to overcome the lies of the enemy and walk in victory and power in Jesus's name! Hallelujah!

How about you? Have you chosen to believe that what Jesus said and did for you is enough to save you from your sin? If not, how about choosing today? Will you confess your sins to Jesus and repent and be healed and set free? If you will, I *know* that Jesus will heal you and restore you and set you free from all loss, pain, fear, and illness, because that is exactly what He did for me! This is the *true* plan of salvation: to choose to place our faith in Jesus Christ alone for our salvation and be healed and set free!

> Wherein in time past ye walked according to the course of this world, according to the prince of the power of the air, the spirit that now worketh in the children of disobedience:[35] Among whom also we all had our conversation in times past in the lusts of our flesh, fulfilling the desires of the flesh and of the mind; and were by nature the children of wrath, even as others.[36] But God, who is rich in mercy, for his great love wherewith he loved us,[37] Even when we were dead in sins, hath quickened us together with Christ, (by grace ye are saved;)[38] And hath raised us up together, and made us sit together in heavenly places in Christ Jesus:

---

[35] See Col. 1:21: "And you, that were sometime alienated and enemies in *your* mind by wicked works, yet now hath he reconciled"

[36] See 1 Pet. 4:3: "For the time past of *our* life may suffice us to have wrought the will of the Gentiles, when we walked in lasciviousness, lusts, excess of wine, revellings, banquetings, and abominable idolatries . . ." See also Gal. 5:16: "*This* I say then, Walk in the Spirit, and ye shall not fulfil the lust of the flesh." See also Ps. 51:5: "Behold, I was shapen in iniquity; and in sin did my mother conceive me."

[37] See Rom. 10:12: "For there is no difference between the Jew and the Greek: for the same Lord over all is rich unto all that call upon him."

[38] See Romans 5:6, 8: "For when we were yet without strength, in due time Christ died for the ungodly. . . . But God commendeth his love toward us, in that, while we were yet sinners, Christ died for us." See also Rom. 6:4, 5: "Therefore we are buried with him by baptism into death: that like as Christ was raised up from the dead by the glory of the Father, even so we also should walk in newness of life. For if we have been planted together in the likeness of his death, we shall be also *in the likeness* of *his* resurrection . . ."

That in the ages to come he might shew the exceeding riches of his grace in his kindness toward us through Christ Jesus. For by grace are ye saved through faith; and that not of yourselves: it is the gift of God: Not of works, lest any man should boast.[39] For we are his workmanship, created in Christ Jesus unto good works, which God hath before ordained that we should walk in them.[40] (Ephesians 2:2–10)

Jesus Christ: Our Living Hope!

God is full of compassion for you and has given you full access to His love through Jesus Christ, who is our living hope! "God is not a man that He should lie" (Numbers 23:19). Once you surrender your life to Jesus Christ by faith, the Holy Spirit seals you to God, and as "the elect of God," you are adopted into the family of God and given an inheritance in the Kingdom of God that will never perish, spoil or fade:

Elect according to the foreknowledge of God the Father, through sanctification of the Spirit, unto obedience and sprinkling of the blood of Jesus Christ: Grace unto you, and peace, be multiplied.[41] Blessed be the God and Father of our Lord Jesus Christ, which according to his abundant mercy hath begotten us again unto a [living]

---

[39] See Rom. 11:6: "And if by grace, then *is it* no more of works: otherwise grace is no more grace. But if *it be* of works, then is it no more grace: otherwise work is no more work." See also Rom. 3:27: "Where *is* boasting then? It is excluded. By what law? of works? Nay: but by the law of faith."

[40] See Isa. 19:25: "Whom the Lord of hosts shall bless, saying, Blessed *be* Egypt my people, and Assyria the work of my hands, and Israel mine inheritance."

[41] See Ephesians. 1:4: "According as he hath chosen us in him before the foundation of the world, that we should be holy and without blame before him in love ..." See also Romans 1:7: "To all that be in Rome, beloved of God, called *to be* saints: Grace to you and peace from God our Father, and the Lord Jesus Christ."

hope by the resurrection of Jesus Christ from the dead,[42] To an inheritance incorruptible, and undefiled, and that fadeth not away, reserved in heaven for you,[43] Who are kept by the power of God through faith unto salvation ready to be revealed in the last time.[44] Wherein ye greatly rejoice, though now for a season, if need be, ye are in heaviness through manifold temptations: That the trial of your faith, being much more precious than of gold that perisheth, though it be tried with fire, might be found unto praise and honour and glory at the appearing of Jesus Christ: Whom having not seen, ye love; in whom, though now ye see him not, yet believing, ye rejoice with joy unspeakable and full of glory:[45] Receiving the end of your faith, even the salvation of your souls. (1 Peter 1:2–9)

---

[42] See John 3:3, 5: "Jesus answered and said unto him, Verily, verily, I say unto thee, Except a man be born again, he cannot see the kingdom of God ... Jesus answered, Verily, verily, I say unto thee, Except a man be born of water and *of* the Spirit, he cannot enter into the kingdom of God." See also 1 Peter 3:21: "The like figure whereunto *even* baptism doth also now save us (not the putting away of the filth of the flesh, but the answer of a good conscience toward God,) by the resurrection of Jesus Christ ..."

[43] See Colossians 1:5: "For the hope which is laid up for you in heaven, whereof ye heard before in the word of the truth of the gospel ..."

[44] See John 10:28: "And I give unto them eternal life; and they shall never perish, neither shall any *man* pluck them out of my hand." See also Philippians. 4:7: "And the peace of God, which passeth all understanding, shall keep your hearts and minds through Christ Jesus."

[45] See 1 John 4:20: "If a man say, I love God, and hateth his brother, he is a liar: for he that loveth not his brother whom he hath seen, how can he love God whom he hath not seen?" See also John 20:29: "Jesus saith unto him, Thomas, because thou hast seen me, thou hast believed: blessed *are* they that have not seen, and *yet* have believed."

A Revelation of Relationship

A life-giving relationship with Jesus Christ by faith is the *key* that will set you free. Once we cross over the valley of unbelief and truly trust Jesus by faith, we will be unstoppable as we walk in powerful victory in Jesus! I am talking about the kind of victory that makes the enemy, Satan, flee from us. Hallelujah! Faith in Jesus Christ will bring a new, deeper level of *joy* that you have never had before, in addition to an overflow of all the supernatural spiritual gifts, or "gifts of the Spirit," identified in 1 Corinthians 12, bringing unity, love, and power to the body of Christ:

> Now concerning spiritual gifts, brethren, I would not have you ignorant. Ye know that ye were Gentiles, carried away unto these dumb idols, even as ye were led. Wherefore I give you to understand, that no man speaking by the Spirit of God calleth Jesus accursed: and that no man can say that Jesus is the Lord, but by the Holy Ghost. Now there are diversities of gifts, but the same Spirit. And there are differences of administrations, but the same Lord. And there are diversities of operations, but it is the same God which worketh all in all. But the manifestation of the Spirit is given to every man to profit withal. For to one is given by the Spirit the word of wisdom; to another the word of knowledge by the same Spirit; To another faith by the same Spirit; to another the gifts of healing by the same Spirit; To another the working of miracles; to another prophecy; to another discerning of spirits; to another divers kinds of tongues; to another the interpretation of tongues: But all these worketh that one and the selfsame Spirit, dividing to every man severally as he will. For as the body is one, and hath many members, and all the members of that one body, being many, are one body: so also is Christ. For by one Spirit are we all baptized into one body, whether we be Jews or Gentiles, whether we

be bond or free; and have been all made to drink into one Spirit. For the body is not one member, but many. If the foot shall say, Because I am not the hand, I am not of the body; is it therefore not of the body? And if the ear shall say, Because I am not the eye, I am not of the body; is it therefore not of the body? If the whole body were an eye, where were the hearing? If the whole were hearing, where were the smelling? But now hath God set the members every one of them in the body, as it hath pleased him. And if they were all one member, where were the body? But now are they many members, yet but one body. And the eye cannot say unto the hand, I have no need of thee: nor again the head to the feet, I have no need of you. Nay, much more those members of the body, which seem to be more feeble, are necessary: And those members of the body, which we think to be less honourable, upon these we bestow more abundant honour; and our uncomely parts have more abundant comeliness. For our comely parts have no need: but God hath tempered the body together, having given more abundant honour to that part which lacked. That there should be no schism [division] in the body; but that the members should have the same care one for another. And whether one member suffer, all the members suffer with it; or one member be honoured, all the members rejoice with it. Now ye are the body of Christ, and members in particular. And God hath set some in the church, first apostles, secondarily prophets, thirdly teachers, after that miracles, then gifts of healings, helps, governments, diversities of tongues. Are all apostles? are all prophets? are all teachers? are all workers of miracles? Have all the gifts of healing? do all speak with tongues? do all interpret? But covet [desire] earnestly the best gifts: and yet shew I unto you a more excellent way.

We see in scripture how to rise up higher out of our fleshly desires to walk in our true spiritual identity—who God created us to be from before the foundation of the world—so that we can become equipped by faith to receive every good gift from the Holy Spirit. It is here in this relationship with Jesus that the "fruit of the Spirit" begins to abound in our lives: "But the fruit of the Spirit is love, joy, peace, longsuffering, gentleness, goodness, faith, Meekness, temperance: against such there is no law" (Galatians 5:22–23).

I hear the sound of victory! Truly, relationship with Jesus Christ is powerful and life-transforming. There is simply nothing like it. The beautiful thing is, once we surrender our lives to Jesus and trust Him with childlike faith, believing our salvation is secure in Him, our hearts, minds, and souls are finally positioned to be aligned with the will of God. We will not have difficulty obeying God's laws and commandments, because we love the Lord with all our hearts, minds, and souls, and His will has become our joy and pleasure (Psalm 119:47). This is how we cooperate with God, allowing the grace of Jesus Christ and the Holy Spirit's power to produce in us the "mind of Christ" (1 Corinthians 2:16). As we feast on the words of Jesus and take the truth of His love for us into our hearts, we won't *want* to rebel or leave His side. This is the key to "righteous living." I like to call this spiritual state "living in the overflow," which refers to living from a place of being loved by Jesus, and thus being fully able to love others. This is the place where joy, peace, rest, abundance, and power flow like a river of life.

Without Faith, We Cannot Please God!

At this point in our journey together, it is vital that you understand that without true faith, we cannot please God! "But without faith it is impossible to please him: for he that cometh to God must believe that he is, and that he is a rewarder of them that diligently seek him" (Hebrews 11:6). We must understand that when we rely on our own ability and strength or on rule keeping, rituals, and ceremonies to make us "righteous" before God, then we are essentially living a works-based faith and are no different than the Jewish Pharisees of Jesus's day! The only thing that counts is faith expressing itself as love (Galatians

5:6). Jesus doesn't want our perfect behavior; He wants our whole hearts. Does this freedom which we have because of the grace Jesus has given us give us license to sin and do whatever we want, to do things contrary to His will or commandments? Absolutely not! The apostle Paul spoke expressly against this kind of rebellion: "What then? shall we sin, because we are not under the law, but under grace? God forbid" (Romans 6:15).

The fact is that if we truly love Jesus, we will no longer choose to sin and rebel, because we are filled with His love. Will we be perfect? No. But the more of Jesus we have inside of our hearts, the less we will desire to sin. If we love Jesus, we will obey the Father, as He did!

Do You Love Me? Feed My Sheep.

The heart of the Father was laid out clearly in what Jesus said to Peter after He appeared to the disciples and spent forty days instructing them:

> So when they had dined, Jesus saith to Simon Peter, Simon, son of Jonas, lovest thou me more than these? He saith unto him, Yea, Lord; thou knowest that I love thee. He saith unto him, Feed my lambs. He saith to him again the second time, Simon, son of Jonas, lovest thou me? He saith unto him, Yea, Lord; thou knowest that I love thee. He saith unto him, Feed my sheep. He saith unto him the third time, Simon, son of Jonas, lovest thou me? Peter was grieved because he said unto him the third time, Lovest thou me? And he said unto him, Lord, thou knowest all things; thou knowest that I love thee. Jesus saith unto him, Feed my sheep. (John 21:15–17)

Jesus is inviting us to show our love for Him by loving others well. In other words, He is saying to us, "Feed my sheep." The Word says that even if you do great things but you have no love in you, you are nothing (1 Corinthians 13:2). The Lord has given us commandments to live by in scripture and tells us that the greatest of these is love (1 Corinthians 13:13

NKJV). The first and greatest commandant is to love the Lord with all your heart and all your soul and all your mind (Deuteronomy 6:5; Matthew 22:36–37). What does it matter if you can "operate" in all nine spiritual gifts identified in 1 Corinthians 12, are flowing in the power of God to perform miracles and healings, and are even able to raise the dead, if you have no love? What if you are operating in a power that appears to be the anointing but you are not operating in love? In the worst cases, a person may be operating out of selfish ambition, malice, envy, hate, or a spirit of murder. In such cases, it is all flesh, and not of the Lord. Jesus said, "Where your treasure is, there your heart will be also" (Matthew 6:21).

What is the condition of *your* heart? In other words, what is the *desire* of your heart? Do you desire to do the will of God and believe Him by faith, obey His Word, and love others well, or do you deny Him and do what you want to do? Words are cheap, and people say all kinds of things they don't actually mean. So what about you? What about me? Do we mean what we say and say what we mean, or are we people-pleasers just following the crowd? Do we really want to obey God, or do we want what *we* want? And what makes us want to do the will of God in the first place? Our ability to obey God is directly correlated to a true, living, and active relationship with Jesus Christ through a personal encounter with Him by the power of the Holy Spirit. Without this, we are just claiming a religion rather than having a true relationship with Jesus Christ! Remember: "We love him, because he first loved us" (1 John 4:19). What a powerful revelation!

Forever Changed!

But how does this revelation of relationship with Jesus happen? God says in Scripture, "Call to me and I will answer you and tell you great and unsearchable things you do not know" (Jeremiah 33:3 NIV). Jesus has promised us that if we cry out to Him with sincere hearts, He will reveal Himself to us! And therein lies the answer: revelation knowledge. We need a revelation of Jesus Christ that seals our hearts to Him by the power of the Holy Spirit. This is what it means to have an "encounter" with the Lord Jesus Christ: a revelation of Him in your heart, soul, and mind that is undeniable and that has the power to change your life forever! This is what happened to me in 2010, and I am forever changed by the love of Jesus! This is possible for you if you desire to truly know Jesus. Again, Jesus desires to be in relationship with you and for you to be set free by His love. This is possible only when we realize that our good works do not equate to relationship and intimacy with the Lord. We must know Him, love Him, and desire Him above everything else with an uncompromising, passionate faith that burns and never goes out. This is what it means to "endure unto the end" (Mark 13:13): to never give up and to never lose your faith, no matter what comes. But the good news is that once we encounter the love and grace of Jesus Christ through a revelation-knowledge encounter, the Holy Spirit seals us to God and we are in the beloved (Song of Solomon 6:3), and He will never forsake us.

The love and grace of Jesus are bigger than our failures. Hallelujah! Once we have tasted the love of Jesus in a truly life-transforming way, we cannot go back to sin and stay there. Why? Because the chains of sin have been broken by the blood of Jesus and the grace that He won for us on the cross, as well as because of the infilling of the Holy Spirit, who has sealed us to God by faith! "In whom ye also trusted, after that ye heard the word of truth, the gospel of your salvation: in whom also after that ye believed, ye were sealed with that holy Spirit of promise" (Ephesians 1:13).

Once we belong to Jesus and His Holy Spirit has sealed us to God, we will not be able to tolerate rebellion for long, because we will know deep in our spirits that we belong to Him and cannot run forever! Just like the prodigal son (see Luke 15:11–32), we will find our way back home even if we choose the *long way home*. I agree with scripture that once we believe in Jesus by faith and have been sealed to God by the power of the Holy Spirit, nothing will be able to separate us from the love of Christ:

> Who shall separate us from the love of Christ? shall tribulation, or distress, or persecution, or famine, or nakedness, or peril, or sword? As it is written, For thy sake we are killed all the day long; we are accounted as sheep for the slaughter. Nay, in all these things we are more than conquerors through him that loved us. For I

am persuaded, that neither death, nor life, nor angels, nor principalities, nor powers, nor things present, nor things to come, Nor height, nor depth, nor any other creature, shall be able to separate us from the love of God, which is in Christ Jesus our Lord. (Romans 8:35–39)

Hallelujah!

Pray with me:

Father, I believe You when You say I am counted righteous by my faith in Jesus Christ and the power of His Blood. I choose today to repent of dead works. I will not trust in my own abilities, but I will fully trust in the finished work of Jesus Christ to make me righteous and justified before You, Father. I know that by Your Holy Spirit, I am sealed to You, and I choose today to believe and live in the confidence that when I repent of my sins and choose to obey your Word, nothing can separate me from Your love. I love You Father, and I trust You completely, in Jesus' name, Amen!

SEVEN

Relationship or Ritual?

And this is life eternal, that they might know thee the only
true God, and Jesus Christ, whom thou hast sent.
—John 17:3

In 2020, I heard the Lord speak something to me in my spirit that almost took my breath away: "Many think they know me, but they don't." Then I thought of Matthew 7:21: "Not every one that saith unto me, Lord, Lord, shall enter into the kingdom of heaven." And then I thought of the somewhat disturbing scripture in verse 23: "I never knew you: depart from me."

What exactly is Jesus saying to us? How do we know if we really know Jesus? Why would Jesus say that some will think they know Him...but actually don't? This verse can cause us to literally quake in our boots until we receive a revelation of the power of a life-giving relationship with Jesus Christ!

I have come to realize that religion is clearly not the same thing as an authentic, personal, chain-breaking, life-altering, transformative relationship with Jesus Christ. I know I am not the only one who has had this revelation. For several years, I had the great blessing of assisting with filming baptism videos at a megachurch in Atlanta. While there, I heard one person after another witness of how they had been raised in a "good Christian home" but never really "knew" Jesus on a personal level. People from ages fourteen to sixty-five shared the same message over and over again: that it was encountering the love and grace of Jesus at a critical time in their lives that became the "game changer" for them. This encounter turned their lukewarm faith into a fiery, life-changing love for Jesus that compelled them to recommit their faith to Jesus and be rebaptized! Can I get a "Hallelujah"? How refreshing it was, and still is, to see a revival hit the hearts of people who *thought* they were in relationship with Jesus out of ritual, who then became alive with the fruit of the Spirit and the power of God! The proof of a true relationship with Jesus is always found in the fruit:

> "But the fruit of the Spirit is love, joy, peace, longsuffering, gentleness, goodness, faith, Meekness, temperance: against such there is no law" (Galatians 5:22–23).

The reality is, human-made religion and religious "laws" will never truly be enough to heal a hurting, wounded heart. In fact, I would argue that human-made religion can bring great damage to people's minds and hearts. Even worse are the effects of heretical cult religion: the leading of well-intentioned people into deception, fear, and control. This is so grievous to the Lord! Adhering to a certain religion will never release the Kingdom keys over your life; only Jesus can do that. Only Jesus holds the keys of death and hell because He alone conquered them, and He alone is worthy. Jesus is inviting you today to receive what He has won for you, and to receive it by faith—not by rule-keeping self-idolatry!

Isn't it astounding that people who *call* themselves believers, even people who attended church all their lives and can quote the Bible backward and forward, can, in actuality, have no real *relationship* with Jesus because they have not encountered His love, mercy, and grace? Encountering Jesus's love, mercy, and grace is the key that opens the way for the Holy Spirit to totally consume us, pouring into us power from heaven. When we have encountered Jesus by the power of the Holy Spirit, nothing can stand against us, for Jesus has opened a door to freedom, joy, victory, and power that no person can shut. When you are born again by a supernatural encounter as a result of true faith overflowing from your heart, nothing can stop you! All hell may try to conspire against you, but it shall not prevail, because the King of Glory, King Jesus, has paid the price in full for your freedom from sin and death and now goes before you, destroying every enemy, every foe, and every evil scheme. Truly, the devil has no power over you! You are free because Jesus has won our freedom at the cross! It is finished! Jesus laid down His life and raised it up for you—He loves you that much! We don't need a baptism certificate, a marriage in a certain building built by humans, or certain phrases or vows or tithes to make us acceptable to God so we can enter heaven. We need pure, undefiled, unadulterated faith in Jesus Christ! The blood of Jesus has the final say. Jesus Christ is the final sacrificial lamb who was slain for our sin, and now we have full access to run to His throne of grace in our time of need.

> Let us therefore come boldly unto the throne of grace, that we may obtain mercy, and find grace to help in time of need. (Hebrews 4:16)

> Having therefore, brethren, boldness to enter into the holiest by the blood of Jesus … Let us draw near with a true heart in full assurance of faith, having our hearts sprinkled from an evil conscience, and our bodies washed with pure water. (Hebrews 10:19, 22)

> For the law made nothing perfect, but the bringing in of a better hope did; by the which we draw nigh unto God. (Hebrews 7:19)[46]

Scripture clearly reveals that we do not need a religion made by man to make us acceptable to God; only the blood of Jesus can do that. All we need is faith in Jesus Christ and His final sacrifice for sin on the cross and a heart open to allowing the Holy Spirit to purify and sanctify us so we can grow from glory to glory, living out our faith from a place of trust and gratitude rather than from fear. The Word of God says, "There

---

[46] See Romans 3:20: "Therefore by the deeds of the law there shall no flesh be justified in his sight: for by the law *is* the knowledge of sin." See also Hebrews 7:7: "And without all contradiction the less is blessed of the better."

is no fear in love" (1 John 4:18). When we truly trust Jesus, we no longer fear, but we can finally *rest*, knowing that we are enough because Jesus is enough!

This is the revelation of relationship I have received and am now spiritually resting in: Jesus Christ is seated at the right hand of God, high and lifted up, because He is the final blood sacrifice that has taken away the sins of the world (Acts 7:55–56; Ephesians 1:20; John 1:29). It is a finished work! I only need to walk in relationship with Him now and trust Him fully for my salvation, knowing I could never ever earn it. Truly we are made right before God and forgiven of our sins through faith in Jesus and His great grace, by which the Holy Spirit now resides in us! The Passion Translation Bible shares the Word of the Lord in a conversational style here:

> But now the Anointed One has become the King-Priest of every wonderful thing that has come. For he serves in a greater, more perfect heavenly tabernacle not made by men, that is to say, not a part of this creation. And he has entered once and forever into the Holiest Sanctuary of All, not with the blood of animal sacrifices, but the sacred blood of his own sacrifice. And he alone has made our salvation secure forever! Under the old covenant the blood of bulls, goats, and the ashes of a heifer were sprinkled on those who were defiled and effectively cleansed them outwardly from their ceremonial impurities. Yet how much more will the sacred blood of the Messiah thoroughly cleanse our consciences! For by the power of the eternal Spirit he has offered himself to God as the perfect Sacrifice that now frees us from our dead works to worship and serve the living God. So Jesus is the One who has enacted a new covenant with a new relationship with God so that those who accept the invitation will receive the eternal inheritance he has promised to his heirs. For he died to release us from the guilt of the violations committed under the first covenant. Now a person's last will and

testament can only take effect after one has been proven to have died; otherwise the will cannot be in force while the person who made it is still alive. So this is why not even the first covenant was inaugurated without the blood of animals. For Moses ratified the covenant after he gave the people all the commandments of the law. He took the blood of calves and goats, with water, scarlet wool, and a hyssop branch, and sprinkled both the people and the book of the covenant, saying,

"This is the blood of the covenant that God commands you to keep."[47]

And later Moses also sprinkled the tabernacle with blood and every utensil and item used in their service of worship. Actually, nearly everything under the law was purified with blood, since forgiveness only comes through an outpouring of blood. And so it was necessary for all the earthly symbols of the heavenly realities to be purified with these animal sacrifices, but the heavenly things themselves required a superior sacrifice than these. For the Messiah did not enter into the earthly tabernacle made by men, which was but an echo of the true sanctuary, but he entered into heaven itself to appear before the face of God in our place. Under the old system year after year the high priest entered the most holy sanctuary with blood that was not his own. But the Messiah did not need to repeatedly offer himself year after year, for that would mean he must suffer repeatedly ever since the fall of the world. But now he has appeared at the fulfillment of the ages to abolish sin once and for all by the sacrifice of himself! Every human being is appointed to die once, and then to face God's judgment. *But when we die we will be face-to-face with Christ,* the One who experienced death once for all to bear the sins of many! And now to those who eagerly await him, he

---

[47]   See Exodus 24:8.

will appear a second time; not to deal with sin, but to bring us the fullness of salvation. (Hebrews 9:11–28)

When believers lack a real relationship with Jesus, they can struggle to cross over the great divide of "dying to self" and choosing to truly live for Jesus. I've seen this over and over again. People desperately want victory, freedom, and joy, and yet they find themselves enslaved to sin and trapped in the fleshly efforts of ritualistic rule-keeping, which will never be able to truly make us secure in our relationship with God. Only a revelation of Jesus and His grace given to us because of His blood poured out for us has the power to do that!

In fact, some people may have gone to church all their lives and still feel totally numb to the things of God. I've been there! The reality is this: we cannot make it to heaven based upon our own religious rule-keeping efforts because we simply cannot ever live our lives that perfectly. I truly believe that it is only when we reach the end of ourselves and realize we will never be enough in our own effort or strength that we will begin to understand what it means to die to self and live for God. This is where true faith begins, and this is when we can *rest*. In other words, when we rely on our own strength and works to make us free or to "be righteous," we are actually living for ourselves and our wills rather than God's will! If you don't know what I mean, I understand, because until I had a revelation of the grace and power of Jesus Christ and His finished work on the cross—the laying down of His life for me and raising it up again—I could not comprehend how my own efforts were really self-worship. But to receive the free gift of salvation by grace through faith and the sealing power of the Holy Spirit is what it means to worship Jesus. He alone is worthy of our worship because He is the only One who holds the keys of sin and death, breaking the chains of bondage from our lives and setting us free to finally live for *Him* and not for ourselves.

It was from this place of dying to myself and what I thought I knew about God that I began the real journey home. The Word of God says it this way: "Verily, verily, I say unto you, Except a corn of wheat fall into the ground and die, it abideth alone: but if it die, it bringeth forth much fruit" (John 12:24).

For us to fully step into our true destinies and become all we are meant to be in the Lord, we must die and live for God! The "breaker anointing" of Jesus Christ (the power of God to deliver, heal, and set free) begins to manifest when you have truly died and been reborn through a relationship with Jesus Christ. It is from this place of choosing relationship by believing in Jesus by faith that we finally rest in Him.

However, if we refuse this truth and continue to struggle and wrestle with our faith, refusing to receive the gift of salvation by faith, we will continue to be in bondage to our own efforts and flesh:

> Let us therefore fear, lest, a promise being left us of entering into his rest, any of you should seem to come short of it. For unto us was the gospel preached, as well as unto them: but the word preached did not profit them, not being mixed with faith in them that heard it. For we which have believed do enter into rest, as he said, As I have sworn in my wrath, if they shall enter into my rest: although the works were finished from the foundation of the world. For he spake in a certain place of the seventh day on this wise, And God did rest the seventh day from all his works. And in this place again, If they shall enter into my rest. Seeing therefore it remaineth that some must enter therein, and they to whom it was first preached entered not in because of unbelief. (Hebrews 4:1–6)

This is stated similarly in The Passion Translation Bible:

> Now the promise of entering into God's rest is still for us today. So we must be extremely careful to ensure that we all embrace the fullness of that promise and not fail to experience it. For we have heard the good news of deliverance just as they did, yet they didn't join their faith with the Word. Instead, what they heard didn't affect them deeply, for they doubted. For those

of us who believe, faith activates the promise and we experience the realm of confident rest! For he has said,
"I was grieved with them and made a solemn oath,
'They will never enter into my rest.'" ...
Those who first heard the good news of deliverance failed to enter into that realm of faith's rest because of their unbelieving hearts. Yet the fact remains that we still have the opportunity to enter into the faith-rest life and experience the fulfillment of the promise! For God still has ordained a day for us to enter into called "Today." For it was long afterwards that God repeated it in David's words,
"If only today you would listen to his voice
and do not harden your hearts!" (Hebrews 4:1–3a, 6–7)

Clearly, when our faith is wrapped up in a works-based belief system, we enter a state of spiritual bondage, being confined to religious boundaries and lines made by man rather than obeying the Lord by faith.

One final issue I feel strongly about addressing is the problem of merchandising the body of Christ. Man-made religion is designed to control people and to make money. How so? Corrupt religious leaders claim that believers must pay money into their "faith" or religion to get into heaven or to receive ministry and the true gospel. Tithing to the church and financial contributions between believers are blessed and Biblical principles (Leviticus 27:30–34; Acts 4:32, 34–35), but sadly, many corrupt church leaders distort those principles. They have allowed greed and profit to direct their ministries, which have become dens of thieves rather than places of true worship. Remember what Jesus did when He went into the temple and saw money changers selling goods in the outer court of the temple? He was furious! He overturned the money changers' tables violently in an act of righteous indignation and exclaimed, "It is written, My house shall be called the house of prayer; but ye have made it a den of thieves" (Matthew 21:13).

We must choose Jesus and submit to the Father's will, just as Jesus did! Jesus Himself said that He came to do the will of the Father (John

6:38). We cannot live for what we want and expect to have the anointing of God upon our lives. We cannot have our "cake" and eat it too! We cannot know Jesus without fully surrendering our lives to *Him*. We must choose to lay down our very lives, sacrificing for the Kingdom of God and His righteousness, just as Jesus did for us! "But seek ye first the kingdom of God, and his righteousness; and all these things shall be added unto you" (Matthew 6:33).

The Pure Anointing

Walking in a relationship with Jesus touches every part of our lives and experiences with God, including the manifestations of the Holy Spirit. I personally have been the recipient of several miracles, including physical and spiritual healings and deliverances by the power of the Holy Spirit. I have also been blessed to be used by the Lord to pray for others and see them be instantly healed. Hallelujah! In the name of Jesus, I have been led by our Lord to cast out demons and to break demonic strongholds on people's lives while praying and ministering to them. I personally have received the Holy Spirit in baptism and now pray in tongues, and I hear the voice of God speaking to me with revelation and the fire of the Holy Spirit on a daily basis. I have also been blessed to witness believers receive the baptism of the Holy Spirit while praying for them, with the evidence of tongues.

Many times, I have experienced the anointing of God so heavily that I was not able to stand! One particular occurrence of this happened at the end of 2019 when Morris Cerullo, who has now gone to be with the Lord, released his anointing to me during a service I attended. He simply reached out to me and touched my forehead with his index finger. I fell so fast I don't remember falling to the ground at all! I was fully aware of myself, and it didn't hurt to fall. I simply rested on the floor under the anointing of God, allowing the Holy Spirit to minister to me! Truly, no harm will come to your body when you are under the anointing! After Cerullo released the anointing to me and I was on the floor under the power of the Almighty God, Cerullo's bodyguard, who was a giant man, nearly seven feet tall, stepped on my thin fingers with the heel of his shoe, but *I did not feel a thing*—not one bit of pain! I was so shocked! It took me about twenty minutes to get up off the floor. I needed assistance from one of the ushers to stand up, and later I needed my friend to help me out to my car when the meeting was over.

All of these examples are both biblical and powerful. We know from the Word of God that Jesus told His disciples that He would send the Holy Spirit to equip them with His power after His ascension to the Father: "But ye shall receive power, after that the Holy Ghost is come upon you: and ye shall be witnesses unto me both in Jerusalem, and in all Judaea, and in Samaria, and unto the uttermost part of the earth" (Acts 1:8).

It truly *is* Biblical for us to receive all that the Holy Spirit wants to do in and through us, and to receive the Holy Spirit by faith! This is exactly what the disciples did on Pentecost, and that same power is available to us today, just as the prophet Joel prophesied: "And it shall come to pass afterward, that I will pour out my spirit upon all flesh; and your sons and your daughters shall prophesy, your old men shall dream dreams, your young men shall see visions: And also upon the servants and upon the handmaids in those days will I pour out my spirit" (Joel 2:28–29).

How wonderful that we can operate in the power of the Holy Spirit because Christ lives in us! When the Holy Spirit enters our tabernacles (bodies) by faith in Jesus Christ, we are fully equipped to operate in the power of God. When we encounter the Holy Spirit in these powerful ways, it is always with the purpose of knowing Jesus more deeply and to empower us to advance His Kingdom, bringing forth victories in the Spirit for God's glory.

While walking in the power of the Holy Spirit, there is a critical discernment we must grow in, which is the discernment of whether a "manifestation" is truly of the Holy Spirit or is from another source. This can be best recognized when people are relying upon their good works, including manifestations of the Spirit, to save them, and claim to operate in the power of God but deny His saving grace and His gospel. When this has occurred, the "power" they are operating in is not of Jesus and His pure anointing but is actually a counterfeit. The Word of God tells us that Satan is always attempting to copy or counterfeit the things of God:

> Satan disguises himself as an angel of light. (2 Corinthians 11:14, NASB 1995)

But though we, or an angel from heaven, preach any other gospel unto you than that which we have preached unto you, let him be accursed. (Galatians 1:8)

If any man love not the Lord Jesus Christ, let him [be accursed]. (1 Corinthians 16:22)

As we said before, so say I now again, If any man preach any other gospel unto you than that ye have received, let him be accursed. (Galatians 1:9)[48]

Often, but not always, I have seen believers seek a "move" of God in miracles, signs, and wonders, but they miss the *real* miracle, sign and wonder: Jesus! Let's look at Matthew 7:22–23: "Many will say to me in that day, Lord, Lord, have we not prophesied in thy name? and in thy name have cast out devils? and in thy name done many wonderful works? And then will I profess unto them, *I never knew you*: depart from me, ye that work iniquity [sin]."[49]

I have learned from experience that the manifestation of gifts and power in the Holy Spirit must be a pure move of God. The issue is this: owing to a lack of spiritual purity and character, not every "move of God" or appearance of God's power comes from a pure anointing. Therefore, we must be very careful how we hear (Mark 4:24; Luke 8:18), evaluate what we experience, and be certain it is from the Holy Spirit. We do this by checking every experience with the Word of God. The sad reality is that not everyone who appears to be operating in the power of the Holy Spirit is *pure*. In fact, some Christians knowingly or unknowingly submit themselves to practicing witchcraft or divination through heretical teachings introduced through wicca, the Harry Potter books and films, Scientology, New Age, Reiki healing, Mormonism, and many other demonic sources of power. This is why it is so important that believers and ministers of the Word remain pure and solely submitted

---

[48] See Deuteronomy 4:2: "Ye shall not add unto the word which I command you, neither shall ye diminish *ought* from it, that ye may keep the commandments of the LORD your God which I command you."

[49] Emphasis added.

to Jesus Christ. If a minister is pure, rooted in a relationship with Jesus Christ by His grace and by the power of the Holy Spirit, then the anointing is pure. But if a minister has not truly encountered the love and grace of Jesus through forgiveness of self and others and has not received the anointing of the Holy Spirit upon them with power, he or she can become corrupted by a heart that has not yet fully matured. Scripture calls this process a "circumcision of the heart" (Deuteronomy 30:6; Romans 2:28–29). Sadly, selfish ambition, pride, manipulation, and control can operate even through people who *claim* to love and know Jesus! When this occurs, it is important to remember that hurting people hurt people, or, in other words, that people who have been hurt, hurt other people—and they don't stop until they have been fully healed by the love of Jesus and the power of the Holy Spirit. If people are operating from anything other than the pure anointing of Jesus Christ, they may not really *know* Jesus, or they may be seeking to know Jesus but have not been purified by the Holy Spirit, and they need to be ministered to for inner healing. In the worst-case scenario, some people who call themselves ministers are simply charlatans and pretenders.

The truth is, in order to minister to others with a pure anointing, we must know Jesus and have a personal relationship with Him that mirrors His heart. We must each develop a knowledge of the Word of God and have a personal encounter with the grace of Jesus and the power of the Holy Spirit in order to develop spiritual wisdom from heaven that will help us discern when a counterfeit power source is present and choose to refuse to cooperate with it. Do not underestimate the damaging effect that a defiled anointing can have on your pure anointing! "Test the spirits" (1 John 4:1–6) and evaluate the spiritual fruit, for you will know these counterfeit sources by their fruits (Matthew 7:16). I can hear you asking, "But how do I know?" The power to discern truth from falsehood is always going to be found from connecting to the vine: Jesus Christ and His Word, straight from the Bible, which is the Word of God.

I am the true vine, and my Father is the husbandman. Every branch in me that beareth not fruit he taketh away: and every branch that beareth fruit, he purgeth it, that it may bring forth more fruit. Now ye are clean through the word which I have spoken unto you. Abide in me, and I in you. As the branch cannot bear fruit of itself, except it abide in the vine; no more can ye, except ye abide in me. I am the vine, ye are the branches: He that abideth in me, and I in him, the same bringeth forth much fruit: for without me ye can do nothing. (John 15:1–5)

A favorite verse of mine is John 17:17: "Sanctify [us] through thy truth: thy word is truth." We can take comfort in knowing that the *true* Word of God, the Bible, will always lead us to the feet of Jesus!

Can We Be Deceived?

So what happens when a person, by the means of man-made religion, only seeks signs, wonders, and miracles? It is very possible that without a pure encounter with Jesus Christ, that person will come under spiritual deception because he or she has taken his or her eyes off of Jesus Christ, the author and finisher of our faith. Matthew 24:4–5 reads, "And Jesus answered and said unto them, Take heed that no man deceive you. For many shall come in my name, saying, I am Christ; and shall deceive many."[50]

And in 1 John 4:1–3, we read, "Beloved, believe not every spirit, but try the spirits whether they are of God: because many false prophets are gone out into the world. Hereby know ye the Spirit of God: Every spirit that confesses that Jesus Christ is come in the flesh is of God:[51] And every spirit that confesses not that Jesus Christ is come in the flesh is

---

[50] See John 5:43: "I am come in my Father's name, and ye receive me not: if another shall come in his own name, him ye will receive."

[51] See Romans 10:8–10: "But what saith it? The word is nigh thee, even in thy mouth, and in thy heart: that is, the word of faith, which we preach; That if thou shalt confess with thy mouth the Lord Jesus, and shalt believe in thine heart that God hath raised him from the dead, thou shalt be saved. For with the heart man believeth unto righteousness; and with the mouth confession is made unto salvation."

not of God: and this is that spirit of antichrist, whereof ye have heard that it should come; and even now already it is in the world."

It is so important we do not give the enemy, who is Satan, a foothold in our lives through which he can enter in and deceive. Instead we must be vigilant to guard our hearts against spiritual deception. I have come to understand and witness how Satan will try to oppose everything that is pure from God by creating a counterfeit to confuse and deceive. Be alert! Be sober! Deception is real, and now more than ever, we need the Holy Spirit to confirm truth to us.

Having been set free from a cult religion, I have found the best way to evaluate any spiritual teaching or experience is to test the validity of what you have seen, experienced, or heard by checking to be sure it agrees with the teachings of Jesus Christ and the Bible. Secondly, we must always pray and ask the Holy Spirit to confirm the truth to us in our *hearts*. Lastly, we must ask God for confirmation to be certain we are understanding God's Word correctly. When we make the effort to read the Word of God straight from the Bible, pray, and seek revelation from the Holy Spirit, we will hear from God! This is how we can and will know truth for *ourselves* and will not be deceived by any counterfeit of the enemy Be comforted in knowing that if you do fall into deception, God will make a way of escape for you if you humble yourself and repent. "There hath no temptation taken you but such as is common to man: but God is faithful, who will not suffer you to be tempted above that ye are able; but will with the temptation also make a way to escape, that ye may be able to bear [endure] it." (1 Corinthians 10:13)

The Lord will always respond to those who desire His will to be done on earth as it is in heaven. As we spend time in the secret place in worship and adoration of Jesus, as well as study in the Word of God, we will understand what it means to live in the will of God. It is from this place of true prayer and humble submission that we will encounter the Living Word, who is Jesus Christ (John 1:1). Spending time with Jesus in the secret place will produce an intimacy with Jesus Christ that will leave you dripping from head to toe in the pure anointing of Jesus. From this intimate place of surrender and love, the power of Jesus and his grace will flow through you as the Holy Spirit comes upon you, producing good fruit that will last! Remember what Jesus himself read from the scrolls of Isaiah:

> The Spirit of the Lord GOD is upon me; because the LORD hath anointed me to preach good tidings unto the meek; he hath sent me to bind up the brokenhearted, to proclaim liberty to the captives, and the opening of the prison to them that are bound; To proclaim the acceptable year of the LORD, and the day of vengeance of our God; to comfort all that mourn; To appoint unto them that mourn in Zion, to give unto them beauty for ashes, the oil of joy for mourning, the garment of praise for the spirit of heaviness; that they might be called trees of righteousness, the planting of the LORD, that he might be glorified. (Isaiah 61:1–3)

Father, help us to never be deceived by seeking only signs and wonders, but may we fall at the feet of Him who is the *true* sign and wonder, Jesus Christ. We ask for the pure anointing to flow through us, producing true miracles, signs and wonders wrought by and through the authority of Jesus Christ by the power of the Holy Spirit.

In Jesus's name,

Amen.

EIGHT

Is God Loving or Harsh?

*For I feared thee, because thou art an austere man: thou takest up
that thou layedst not down, and reapest that thou didst not sow.*
—Luke 19:21

Over the years, I have found that many people struggle to believe
that God really wants a relationship with them and to believe that
He is a loving God and not a harsh taskmaster who is waiting to punish
them for their sins. If we read Luke 19:21 without revelation from the
Holy Spirit, it would appear that God is, in fact, harsh and to be feared.
This perspective does not agree with the many verses of scripture that
tell us that God is love and that if we know God we will love God and
be loved by Him:

> He that loveth not knoweth not God; for God is love. (1
> John 4:8)

> There is no fear in love; but perfect love casteth out fear:
> because fear hath torment. He that feareth is not made
> perfect in love. We love him, because he first loved us.
> (1 John 4: 18–19)

Some believers struggle to truly believe that God's love is
unconditional. But that is just what Scripture tells us! God has a good
plan for our lives, for those who love Him and who are called according
to His purpose (Romans 8:28). When we have given our hearts to Jesus

and are living for Him by faith, we must expect a good outcome and a favorable end. I truly believe that when we choose to place our faith in Jesus Christ alone for our salvation, we have the promise of God's Word to hold on to, so that even when the winds and storms of life come against our faith, His Word sustains our hope and trust in God's goodness, mercy, and love:

> Blessed be the God and Father of our Lord Jesus Christ, which according to his abundant mercy hath begotten us again unto a lively hope by the resurrection of Jesus Christ from the dead,[52] To an inheritance incorruptible, and undefiled, and that fadeth not away, reserved in heaven for you.[53] (1 Peter 1:3–4)

When we read scripture from a perspective of the goodness of God, believing that His intentions toward us are good and not evil, our faith will deepen as we rest in this truth. From this place of rest and trust, our faith will rise up to a higher level of authority and power as the Holy Spirit confirms the Word of God in our hearts! But if we become like the Pharisees of Jesus's day, then we will be tempted to operate as "religious" people of unbelief—people who focus on "measuring up to God's expectations" out of righteous deeds and rule-keeping rituals rather than developing a personal relationship with Jesus Christ. Remember that pride comes before the fall (Proverbs 16:18)! But if we trust in the love of God the Father through knowing Jesus Christ His son, and honor Him, we will have rest and peace in our hearts:

---

[52] See John 3:3, 5: "Jesus answered and said unto him, Verily, verily, I say unto thee, Except a man be born again, he cannot see the kingdom of God … Jesus answered, Verily, verily, I say unto thee, Except a man be born of water and *of* the Spirit, he cannot enter into the kingdom of God." See also 1 Peter 3:21: "The like figure whereunto *even* baptism doth also now save us (not the putting away of the filth of the flesh, but the answer of a good conscience toward God,) by the resurrection of Jesus Christ …"

[53] See Colossians 1:5: "For the hope which is laid up for you in heaven, whereof ye heard before in the word of the truth of the gospel …"

For the Father loveth the Son, and sheweth him all things that himself doeth: and he will shew him greater works than these, that ye may marvel.[54] For as the Father raiseth up the dead, and quickeneth [gives life to] *them*; even so the Son quickeneth whom he will. For the Father judgeth no man, but hath committed all judgment unto the Son:[55] That all *men* should honour the Son, even as they honour the Father. He that honoureth not the Son honoreth not the Father which hath sent him.[56] (John 5:20–3)

In Luke 19:11–27, Jesus shares with us a parable that, when discerned with revelation from the Holy Spirit, reveals the heart of God: that He desires to bless us and not condemn us. In fact, this parable reveals that it is not God's disappointment or anger that brings judgment, but rather *the lack of faith* found in the unprofitable servant that renders judgment.

Jesus begins by telling the story of a nobleman who had gone on a journey and left talents, or money, to his servants. To the first he gave ten talents; to the second, five; and to the third, one. Upon returning, the nobleman took an account of what his servants had done with the talents he had given them to steward.

In the telling of the parable of the talents, I believe Jesus is demonstrating that God does not desire to punish us but rather cares about us receiving and using by faith what He has given us. God will respond to our genuine faith and how we view *His* character over our performance every time! But if we choose not to believe God is for us, then we are in sin, because this is *unbelief*!

And it came to pass, that when [the nobleman] was returned, having received the kingdom, then he

---

[54]   See John 3:35: "The Father loveth the Son, and hath given all things into his hand."

[55]   See Matthew 11:27: "All things are delivered unto me of my Father: and no man knoweth the Son, but the Father; neither knoweth any man the Father, save the Son, and *he* to whomsoever the Son will reveal *him*."

[56]   See 1 John 2:23: "Whosoever denieth the Son, the same hath not the Father: (but) he that acknowledgeth the Son hath the Father also.*"*

commanded these servants to be called unto him, to whom he had given the money, that he might know how much every man had gained by trading. Then came the first, saying, Lord, thy pound hath gained ten pounds. And he said unto him, Well, thou good servant: because thou hast been faithful in a very little, have thou authority over ten cities. And the second came, saying, Lord, thy pound hath gained five pounds. And he said likewise to him, Be thou also over five cities. And another came, saying, Lord, behold, *here is* thy pound, which I have kept laid up in a napkin: For I feared thee, because thou art an austere man: thou takest up that thou layedst not down, and reapest that thou didst not sow. And he saith unto him, Out of thine own mouth will I judge thee, *thou* wicked servant. Thou knewest that I was an austere man, taking up that I laid not down, and reaping that I did not sow: Wherefore then gavest not thou my money into the bank, that at my coming I might have required mine own with usury? And he said unto them that stood by, Take from him the pound, and give *it* to him that hath ten pounds. (And they said unto him, Lord, he hath ten pounds.) For I say unto you, That unto every one which hath shall be given; and from him that hath not, even that he hath shall be taken away from him. But those mine enemies, which would not that I should reign over them, bring hither, and slay them before me. (Luke 19:15–27)

Notice verse 21: "for I feared thee, because thou art an austere man: thou takest up that thou layedst [lay] not down, and reapest that thou didst not sow." The servant reveals his corrupt heart, accusing the nobleman of being "austere," or severe, stern, harsh, and too strict. What would compel this steward of the nobleman to make such an assumption? The answer is fear and unbelief about the goodness of the character of the nobleman!

Have we not made this same mistake about the nature and heart of God? Do we not sometimes fear that God wants to punish us when we miss the mark, sin, fall down, or are out of agreement with His will? The truth of God's character is seen vividly here in one of the most commonly quoted verses in the Bible: "For God so loved the world, that he gave his only begotten Son, that whosoever believeth in him should not perish, but have everlasting life" (John 3:16).

If God's heart is that none should perish, does he allow some to miss heaven and live forever in eternal punishment? Is God a loving Father, or is He a harsh taskmaster, reaping where He did not sow? Countless examples in the Word show that God's desire is that all mankind would be saved, but He doesn't force us to be! Take the parable of the prodigal son, for example (Luke 15:11–32), or the story of Jesus ministering to the Samaritan woman at the well (John 4:5–26). In both cases, we see a stunning demonstration of God's heart for the sinner!

Even though God's thoughts toward us are good and full of love and compassion, God still loves us enough to allow us to decide how we want to view His heart for us. In other words, we can choose to believe God is for us, or we can choose to believe He is against us. Our attitudes about God's character show up in how we speak about God and His intentions toward us. A good example of this heart condition is seen in Luke 19:22, which takes us to a cross reference verse in 2 Samuel 1:16. As we look at the latter verse, we see that God weighs our words. Through these verses, He identifies the real problem: a declaration of unbelief, or refusal to believe, that God is full of love, grace, mercy, and justice. The Word of God reveals that this unbelief is actually *rebellion!* What we say and think about God matters a great deal to Him because it reveals our hearts and whether we possess true faith or not!

> And David said unto him, Thy blood *be* upon thy head; for thy mouth hath testified against thee. (2 Samuel 1:16)

> And he saith unto him, Out of thine own mouth will I judge thee, thou wicked servant. (Luke 19:22)

Truly, "out of the abundance of the heart the mouth speaks." (Matthew 12:34, NKJV)[57]

The wicked servant revealed that his heart was full of unbelief by declaring with his own mouth that God is a harsh taskmaster. The servant doubted God's goodness and expected that God would be harsh with him, and he declared his denial of the true character of God's heart, resulting in rebellion against God.

In this parable, the Lord is revealing that the declaration of unbelief that came out of the mouths of those who slandered and blasphemed God brought their condemnation. Would a blood-bought covenant believer of Jesus Christ really do this? I do not believe so! Let this revelation from the Word of God rest upon your spirit now: God does not desire to cast you into hell when you sin and "fall down." However, God does ask us to repent when we have sinned in order to restore our relationships with Him and others we have harmed. God *will* deal with the sin of unbelief and rebellion against His character, but God can work with true faith and will minister to our faith as we choose to believe God is love and wants to give us a hope and a future, and that His is plans for us are good.

Manifesting the Glory of God!

If we are honest, we have all experienced some level of failure and sin, because we are all human. And then what? What happens next? I believe personal failure is the training ground to be prepared to be used by God for His glory! Why? Because God loves to restore broken hearts! When we put down our shame and pick up our faith instead, we become positioned to receive the blessings of God. As real faith arises, the true, manifested sons of God arise with freedom, joy, and the anointing of the Holy Spirit: "For the earnest expectation of the creature waiteth for the manifestation of the sons of God. For the creature was made subject to vanity, not willingly, but by reason of him who hath subjected *the*

---

[57]   See Luke 6:45: "A good man out of the good treasure of his heart bringeth forth that which is good; and an evil man out of the evil treasure of his heart bringeth forth that which is evil: for of the abundance of the heart his mouth speaketh."

same in hope, Because the creature itself also shall be delivered from the bondage of corruption into the glorious liberty of the children of God" (Romans 8:19–21).

These verses lead us to Galatians, which teaches us about breaking free from the bondage of the law and religious behavior and entering into true freedom, joy, and power from the Lord. Remember, "the joy of the LORD is your strength" (Nehemiah 8:10)!

> Stand fast therefore in the liberty wherewith Christ hath made us free, and be not entangled again with the yoke of bondage. (Galatians 5:1)

> For, brethren, ye have been called unto liberty; only *use* not liberty for an occasion to the flesh, but by love serve one another. (Galatians 5:13)

The manifested sons of God are those who will rise up in faith and manifest the glory of the goodness of God in their lives because Jesus Christ has set them free from the bondage of sin and the flesh, and God has delivered them from the dominion of darkness into the Kingdom of His Son: "[God] hath delivered us from the power of darkness, and hath translated *us* into the kingdom of his dear Son" (Colossians 1:13).[58]

When we encounter the love of God through His Son, Jesus Christ, by the power of the Holy Spirit, we can truly be set free from the dominion of darkness and brought into the Kingdom of God's Son! This is God's heart for each of us: that we would be *set free* and operate in the anointing of Jesus Christ by the power of the Holy Spirit! It is so grievous to the Lord when He has offered us authority, power, anointing, giftings, forgiveness, and grace and we refuse to receive it.

---

[58] See Ephesians 6:12: "For we wrestle not against flesh and blood, but against principalities, against powers, against the rulers of the darkness of this world, against spiritual wickedness in high *places*." See also 2 Peter 1:11: "For so an entrance shall be ministered unto you abundantly into the everlasting kingdom of our Lord and Saviour Jesus Christ."

When we surrender our hearts to receiving a loving relationship with Jesus, we begin to live life out of a genuine overflow of love for the Lord that enables us to consistently obey his Word, more and more. As we begin to obey God's words, believing in His goodness, grace, mercy, and love for the sinner, and live our lives from the overflow of a personal relationship with Jesus, we will finally begin to enter divine rest and trust, and be free! Read over these verses about loving God and obeying His commandment to believe in Him and trust in Him with all of our hearts:

> If ye love me, keep my commandments. (John 14:15)

> For this is the love of God, that we keep his commandments: and his commandments are not grievous. (1 John 5:3)

> Come unto me, all *ye* that labour and are heavy laden, and I will give you rest. Take my yoke upon you, and learn of me; for I am meek and lowly in heart: and ye shall find rest unto your souls.[59] For my yoke *is* easy, and my burden is light. (Matthew 11:28–30)

> For we walk by faith, not by sight. (2 Corinthians 5:7)

> For we are saved by hope: but hope that is seen is not hope: for what a man seeth, why doth he yet hope for? (Romans 8:24)[60]

> Now faith is the substance of things hoped for, the evidence of things not seen. (Hebrews 11:1)

> And Jesus said unto them, I am the bread of life: he that cometh to me shall never hunger; and he that believeth

---

[59] See John 13:15: "For I have given you an example, that ye should do as I have done to you."

[60] See Romans 4:18: "Who against hope believed in hope, that he might become the father of many nations, according to that which was spoken, So shall thy seed be."

on me shall never thirst.[61] But I said unto you, That ye also have seen me, and believe not.[62] All that the Father giveth me shall come to me; and him that cometh to me I will in no wise cast out. (John 6:35–7)[63]

It is written in the prophets, And they shall be all taught of God. Every man therefore that hath heard, and hath learned of the Father, cometh unto me. (John 6:45)

And I give unto them eternal life; and they shall never perish, neither shall any man pluck them out of my hand. My Father, which gave them to me, is greater than all; and no man is able to pluck them out of my Father's hand. (John 10:28–29)

Jesus wants a relationship with you, and He is willing to meet you where you are in your journey and heal you. Jesus, who is one with the Father, is full of grace and mercy for the sinner. He simply asks you to believe in Him by faith and place your trust in Him alone. Choose today to receive the grace to trust Jesus more!

---

[61] See John 4:14: "But whosoever drinketh of the water that I shall give him shall never thirst; but the water that I shall give him shall be in him a well of water springing up into everlasting life." See also John 6:48, 58: "I am that bread of life ... This is that bread which came down from heaven: not as your fathers did eat manna, and are dead: he that eateth of this bread shall live for ever." See also John 7:37: "In the last day, that great *day* of the feast, Jesus stood and cried, saying, If any man thirst, let him come unto me, and drink."

[62] See John 6:26, 64: "Jesus answered them and said, Verily, verily, I say unto you, Ye seek me, not because ye saw the miracles, but because ye did eat of the loaves, and were filled ... But there are some of you that believe not. For Jesus knew from the beginning who they were that believed not, and who should betray him." See also John 10:26: "But ye believe not, because ye are not of my sheep, as I said unto you." See also John 15:24: "If I had not done among them the works which none other man did, they had not had sin: but now have they both seen and hated both me and my Father."

[63] See 1 John 2:19: "They went out from us, but they were not of us; for if they had been of us, they would *no doubt* have continued with us: but *they went out*, that they might be made manifest that they were not all of us."

NINE

To See the Kingdom of God, Be Born Again!

Jesus answered and said unto him, Verily, verily I say unto thee,
Except a man be born again, he cannot see the kingdom of God.
—John 3:3

We are all in need of some kind of healing, whether it be physical, emotional, or spiritual. When we have open hearts and allow the Holy Spirit to minister to our brokenness, we will be able to receive the healing we've been longing for. During Jesus's ministry, a very religious and well-respected rabbi named Nicodemus was curious about Jesus and sought to meet with Him. He had seen how Jesus ministered to the people and was aware of the miracles that had occurred, so he did what an intelligent and responsible follower of God would do: he pursued a private meeting with Jesus. In this unique meeting, Jesus unveiled one of the greatest mysteries of the Kingdom: the nature of the Holy Spirit. Though Nicodemus was a Jewish rabbi and was recognized as a minister of the Word of God who most likely lived life by a set of very structured rules, regulations, and discipline, I can't help but think that he must have been yearning for something more. Perhaps he was confused as to how this Jesus could perform such powerful miracles and was looking for answers. Maybe he wanted to seek out Jesus for more personal reasons. Scripture doesn't say. But what we do see in scripture is what Jesus said about the Holy Spirit and what it means to be "born again":

> Jesus answered and said unto him, Verily, verily I say unto thee, Except a man be born again, he cannot see the kingdom of God. (John 3:3)

> Which were born, not of blood, nor of the will of the flesh, nor of the will of man, but of God. (John 1:13)

Then Nicodemus asked this question of Jesus: "How can a man be born when he is old? can he enter the second time into his mother's womb, and be born?" (John 3:4). Jesus gives what must have been a perplexing response: "Verily, verily, I say unto thee, Except a man be born of water and of the Spirit, he cannot enter into the kingdom of God" (John 3:5).[64]

I can only imagine the questions that must have been running through Nicodemus's mind as he pondered Jesus's compelling words! Born of water *and the Spirit*? How can a person come out of the womb a second time? The literal meaning simply doesn't make sense. For someone who had built his entire faith around rule keeping and rituals, imagine how absolutely out of his comfort zone it must have been for Nicodemus to even entertain the thought that there could be a way to be "born again" in the Spirit. This must have seemed so *foreign* to him! In fact, his bewilderment shows us that the mysteries of the Kingdom cannot be understood by our rational minds, by logic. Only though revelation knowledge by the power of the Holy Spirit could Nicodemus, or any of us, understand the mysteries of God—which is the very reason why we must understand the Holy Spirit and seek to know Him! Jesus tells us that as we do so, He will baptize us with the fire of the Holy Spirit, who gives us revelation knowledge (Matthew 3:11; Luke 3:16). Only then can we know the mysteries of the Kingdom of God!

The Word does not tell us much about what happened after Nicodemus's meeting with Jesus. Did the Holy Spirit come upon him, or did he walk away frustrated and confused? Honestly, any time we

---

64   See Mark 16:16: "He that believeth and is baptized shall be saved; but he that believeth not shall be damned." See also Acts 2:38: "Then Peter said unto them, Repent, and be baptized every one of you in the name of Jesus Christ for the remission of sins, and ye shall receive the gift of the Holy Ghost."

enter new and unfamiliar territory in life, it is normal to feel somewhat apprehensive or cautious, right? Jesus had made a bold statement, and Nicodemus may not have been ready to receive it. We do know that Jesus revealed that Nicodemus's faith was limited by a lack of understanding and revelation: "Nicodemus answered and said unto him, How can these things be? Jesus answered and said unto him, Art thou a master of Israel, and knowest not these things? Verily, verily, I say unto thee, we speak that we do know, and testify that we have seen; and ye receive not our witness. If I have told you earthly things, and ye believe not, how shall ye believe, if I tell you of heavenly things?" (John 3:9–12).

We can all learn a powerful lesson from examining this story from scripture. Nicodemus, hungry and seeking truth, ended up empty-handed even though Jesus Christ, the true Messiah, was standing right before his very eyes! This story for me is a great example of what can happen when we rely upon logic rather than revelation. This is why we need to allow the Holy Spirit to reveal the mysteries of God to us. Placing our faith in Jesus is just the beginning of the spiritual journey! As we continue to abide in Jesus and develop our faith in Him and allow our hearts to be processed by the Holy Spirit's power, we will eventually become the anointed, chain-breaking, powerful men and women of God that He has called us to be. When we receive the baptism of the Holy Spirit and allow Him to refine us and to act through us, we grow into knowing what it is to operate in the power and authority of God! Once we open our hearts to receiving Jesus as the Lord of our lives, we enter the process of sanctification of the Holy Spirit. As we allow the Holy Spirit to move freely in and upon us, the anointing from Jesus Christ will break every yoke of spiritual bondage. Some refer to this move of God as the "breaker anointing," which will loose us from bondage, transforming us from "glory to glory" (2 Corinthians 3:18). One of my favorite lines of scripture is what Jesus said to the woman who had a spirit of infirmity for eighteen years: "Daughter, be loosed"—or, in other words, "Be healed and set free": "And, behold, there was a woman which had a spirit of infirmity eighteen years, and was bowed together, and could in no wise lift up herself. And when Jesus saw her, he called her to him, and said unto her, Woman, thou art loosed from thine infirmity. And he laid his hands on her: and immediately she was made straight, and glorified God" (Luke 13:11–13).

For the anointing of Jesus Christ to operate, the Holy Spirit must also be present and operating. Jesus reveals this truth to us when he said something very radical by relating the Spirit to wind: "The wind bloweth where it listeth [wishes], and thou hearest the sound thereof, but canst not tell whence it cometh, and whither it goeth: so is every one that is born of the Spirit.[65] Nicodemus answered and said unto him, How can these things be?"[66] (John 3:8–9).

During my own search for truth, I found many Christians are asking the very same question today about the Holy Spirit: "How can these things be?" Honestly, my heart goes out to anyone searching for truth, because I know what it feels like to be searching for answers while feeling like you are coming up short. Until the Holy Spirit opens our eyes to the mysteries of God, there are simply some things we cannot perceive with the analytical, natural, or human mind. But the good news is, once we are saved by faith and allow the Holy Spirit to move freely in and through us, we will have full access to the power of the Holy Spirit in our lives through a relationship with Jesus Christ. Then we will be equipped with power from God to do what Jesus did: operate under the direction of the Holy Spirit to set the captives free. After, all God's love and power is more available to us than we ever could have imagined!

Prior to my experiencing the baptism of the Holy Spirit, as I now understand it to be called, I had never been taught that the Holy Spirit could come upon me with power (Acts 1:8), but we know from scripture that that is precisely what Jesus declared when He read Isaiah 61:1–3, which was later recalled in Luke 4:18: "The Spirit of the Lord is upon me, because he hath anointed me to preach the gospel to the poor; he hath sent me to heal the brokenhearted, to preach deliverance to the captives, and recovering of sight to the blind, to set at liberty them that are bruised."

---

[65] See 1 Corinthians 2:11: "For what man knoweth the things of a man, save the spirit of man which is in him? even so the things of God knoweth no man, but the Spirit of God."

[66] See John 6:52, 60 "The Jews therefore strove among themselves, saying, How can this man give us *his* flesh to eat? ... Many therefore of his disciples, when they had heard *this*, said, This is an hard saying; who can hear it?"

The baptism of the Holy Spirit is absolutely needed to be able to minister with the anointing of Jesus Christ. Does this mean that believers cannot pray or operate in their spiritual gifts without the baptism of the Holy Spirit? My answer is twofold: yes, you can still minister, but the effectiveness and result may not be the same. For example, if you are going to pray for someone to be healed, wouldn't you want to see the healing occur? If you are praying for someone to be set free from demonic oppression, wouldn't you want to see the result? If so, you cannot accomplish that kind of powerful ministry without the baptism of the Holy Spirit, because these very things cannot happen without God's power! In fact, I believe this is the very reason why so many churches exist today without the evidence of God's power; they overlooked the need for the power of God to move freely and have quenched the Holy Spirit. In some cases, churches have gone so far as to eliminate teaching on the baptism of the Holy Spirit from their doctrines entirely!

Prior to my encounter with the Lord, I had never been taught about the baptism of the Holy Spirit and did not know anything about the anointing of Jesus, enabling a believer to operate with power (Acts 1:8). Sadly, I was indoctrinated to believe that the only way a person could receive the Holy Spirt was by the laying on of hands by the spiritual elders of my church that I was attending at that time. According to this church, these elders could only be men, and absolutely no woman could have access to the power of God without an elder in the church laying hands upon her to impart the Holy Spirit. What control! Additionally, women simply were not considered able to administer the anointing of the Holy Spirit; they could only receive. So, naturally, I was predisposed to believe women were limited in how they could minister in the Kingdom of God until the Holy Spirit came upon me and anointed me with a powerful breaker anointing to set the captives free, because that is exactly with Jesus Christ did for me!

You can only imagine my utter shock and surprise when the power of God came upon me in 2010, setting me free from a false religion, healing my body from three autoimmune diseases, and delivering me from demonic strongholds and from being abused. Later, in 2015, I experienced a second powerful impartation of the Holy Spirit during the first women's ministry retreat that I planned and facilitated, in which I was equipped and anointed with the power of the Holy Spirit. The result was nothing short of miraculous as we saw physical healing, the casting out of demons, deep spiritual freedom, and an immense impartation of joy!

How wonderful that Jesus instructed believers in both the "anointing" (Isaiah 61:1) as well as in being "born again" (John 3:3). Prior to being taught anything about these doctrines, I personally experienced a life-changing, chain-breaking encounter with the Holy Spirit that set me free from the generational bondage of cult religion as well as the terrible effects of abuse and corruption of the mind. On both occasions, the Holy Spirit came upon me and powerfully anointed me for the ministry. Afterward, I was transformed spiritually: I had been totally changed by and filled with the Holy Spirit, and I was later anointed by God to minister with power to the Glory of God. Hallelujah!

Honestly, I feel it is nothing short of a tragedy that some believers preach against the equipping power of God through the baptism of the Holy Spirit. I believe what people do not realize is that the Holy Spirit is a member of the Trinity, is one with both the Father and Jesus Christ, and is to be respected, honored, cherished, and loved—*not quenched.* In fact, we see the baptism of the Holy Spirit verified through the testimony of Apostle Paul, who received the baptism of the Holy Spirit as described in the book of Acts. Here we see from scripture that the Lord spoke to Ananias and instructed him to go and pray for Paul, who had just encountered the Lord Jesus Christ on the road to Damascus. Paul was in need of prayer and deliverance, and the Lord assigned Ananias to be the vessel to pray for Paul so he could rise up to answer God's call on his life and fulfill his destiny to preach the gospel of Jesus Christ with power and authority of the Holy Spirit:

> And there was a certain disciple at Damascus, named Ananias; and to him said the Lord in a vision, Ananias. And he said, Behold, I am here, Lord. And the Lord said unto him, Arise, and go into the street which is called Straight, and enquire in the house of Judas for one called Saul, of Tarsus: for, behold, he prayeth, And hath seen in a vision a man named Ananias coming in, and putting his hand on him, that he might receive his sight.

Then Ananias answered, Lord, I have heard by many of this man, how much evil he hath done to thy saints at Jerusalem: And here he hath authority from the chief priests to bind all that call on thy name. But the Lord said unto him, Go thy way: for he is a chosen vessel unto me, to bear my name before the Gentiles, and kings, and the children of Israel: For I will shew him how great things he must suffer for my name's sake. And Ananias went his way, and entered into the house; and putting his hands on him said, Brother Saul, the Lord, even Jesus, that appeared unto thee in the way as thou camest, hath sent me, that thou mighest receive thy sight, *and be filled with the Holy Ghost.* And immediately there fell from his eyes as it had been scales: and he received sight forthwith, and arose, and was baptized. (Acts 9:10–18, emphasis added)

Here we clearly see that Paul received the baptism of the Holy Spirit through the laying on of hands from Ananias, who was a minister of God. Paul received Ananias and allowed him to pray so that he could receive the baptism of the Holy Spirit with power. Later, Saul, who became Apostle Paul, was able to minister to unbelievers with the power and authority of Jesus Christ! Interestingly, we also see in scripture that Paul was baptized with water *after* receiving the baptism of the Holy Spirit. The timing of the two events is not significant, but the fact that there exists two baptisms *is.*

Finally, we see evidence from scripture that after Paul received the baptism of the Holy Spirit, he was able to minister with power, boldness, and authority:

And when he had received meat, he was strengthened. Then was Saul certain days with the disciples which were at Damascus. And straightway he preached Christ in the synagogues, that he is the Son of God ... But Barnabas took him, and brought him to the apostles, and declared unto them how he had seen the Lord in the way, and that he had spoken to him, and how he had preached boldly at Damascus in the name of Jesus. And he was with them coming in and going out at Jerusalem. And he spake boldly in the name of the Lord Jesus, and disputed against the Grecians ... (Acts 9:19–20, 27–9)

What about you? After reading clear evidence straight from the Word of God, are you open to receiving the baptism of the Holy Spirit? Do you want to be like Nicodemus, a religious Pharisee, or like Apostle Paul, a bold and powerful minister who wrote more than half of the New Testament, leading nations to Christ? The choice is yours. You can choose today to break rank, parting ways with religious traditions, and instead ask the Holy Spirit to pour out His power on you so that you can fulfill your God-given destiny!

What About Speaking in Tongues?

When we are awakened to the realm of the Holy Spirit, we find ourselves experiencing His power and revelation as He reveals the character and heart of Jesus to us. Additionally, the Holy Spirit will awaken us to dormant spiritual gifts we have been given from the Father that we may not have discovered yet! There are nine spiritual gifts that are identified in 1 Corinthians 12:4–10:

Now there are diversities of gifts, but the same Spirit. And there are differences of administrations, but the same Lord. And there are diversities of operations, but it is the same God which worketh all in all. But the manifestation of the Spirit is given to every man to profit withal. For to one is given by the Spirit the word of wisdom; to another the word of knowledge by the same Spirit; To another faith by the same Spirit; to another the gifts of healing by the same Spirit; To another the working of miracles; to another prophecy; to another discerning of spirits; to another divers kinds of tongues; to another the interpretation of tongues ...

Praying in tongues is a spiritual gift, and it is available to everyone, but it is not the *only* evidence of having the baptism of the Holy Spirit, as it is a *gift* of the Spirit. Scripture does tell us that in one instance, God allowed a Roman centurion and his family to pray in tongues as a sign to Peter that they, in fact, had been baptized in the Holy Ghost (Acts 10:1–11:18). Peter may have needed a sign from God so that his faith could rise up to accept that God shows no favoritism and will pour out His Spirit upon whomever He chooses. However, this story should not be used to argue that everyone must speak in tongues to *prove* he or she has the baptism of the Holy Spirit; it should rather be viewed as a sign that the baptism of the Holy Spirit has occurred in a believer's life.

One of the most known examples of the baptism of the Holy Spirit is found in Acts 2, when the Holy Spirit comes upon the disciples, baptizing them with the Holy Spirit. Cloven tongues of fire appear before them, and they all pray in tongues (Acts 2:3–4). This, too, was a sign of God's presence through a manifestation of the Holy Spirit coming upon them. So, when believers pray in the language of the angels, or in "tongues," we can receive it as evidence that God's presence has come upon them with power through the Holy Spirit, remembering that praying in tongues is a gift—though it is not a requirement for salvation! Still, knowing that praying in tongues can allow us to pray the language of the angels (1 Corinthians 13:1) and help our prayers to line up with God's perfect will (Romans 8:26) should cause us all to desire this wonderful gift.

Lastly, as we allow the Holy Spirit to fill us, we become what scripture calls a "habitation of the Lord" (see Ephesians 2:22), just at the Old Testament temple was for the people of Israel: "What? know ye not that your body is the temple of the Holy Ghost which is in you, which ye have of God, and ye are not your own?" (1 Corinthians 6:19).

Today the Holy Spirit desires not just visitation but also "habitation" inside of you, to equip you with every good gift from heaven! He wants to confirm to you the Word, who is Jesus Christ. If you have not yet encountered the tangible power of the baptism of the Holy Spirit, I pray you will open your heart to receive this wonderful gift and blessing over your life today! Now more than ever, we need the spiritual equipping of the Holy Spirit to discern the signs and the times we are living in. When the Holy Spirit awakens us to the realm of the Spirit, we will find ourselves experiencing empowered walks with Jesus. Then, as the Holy Spirit washes and regenerates our spirits as a result of our faith in Jesus, He has permission to baptize us with power, just as he did for the apostles on Pentecost (Acts 2)!

Oftentimes, experiencing a movement of the Holy Spirit can challenge one's current level of faith. When I first heard a believer pray in tongues, I was so shocked and thought, "What in the *world* is *that*?" I even prayed, "Lord, I believe; help my unbelief!" Later, when I sought to learn more about it, I realized that we can all pray in tongues if we want to. So, one summer evening, I sought the Lord and asked Him whether He would give me the gift of praying in tongues. Immediately I heard an unrecognizable phrase run through my mind. It was so subtle that I thought I was imagining things. Then, I heard the same phrase again. At this point, I started to feel excited in my spirit as I realized the Lord had answered my prayer—I was hearing a foreign language! So I did the funniest thing—I tried to write down what I heard phonetically! The temptation to doubt that I had heard from the Lord crept in on me, and I wasn't sure. I wondered, "Did the Holy Spirit just give me tongues?" I said to Jesus, "If that was you, Lord, make me remember it again in the future." I snapped my notebook shut and forgot about it.

Two months later, I was facilitating a women's retreat and was praying for a woman who had been severely abused as a child. She was really in need of help. I started to feel overwhelmed about how to help her, but then I heard the Holy Spirit say to me, "Pray the phrase I gave you." I said to myself, "I don't remember it!" and then—*Pow!*—The words came rolling off my tongue, with the dialect and inflection of a completely different language—one I had never spoken before! I was very shy about it. I prayed so softly that it was hardly audible. But then, as I prayed in tongues, the woman began to be delivered from the power of the enemy, and those demons began to flee. Hallelujah! After we were done, she said to me, "You were praying in tongues!" I said, "Was I?" She answered, "Yes, Ashley, you were!" This woman proceeded to share with me that she once worked in the office of Oral Roberts Ministries and that she knew all about praying in tongues. Wow! God is so good!

What I hope you will understand from my sharing of this story is this: just as salvation cannot be earned, we cannot be "born again" out of a place of "performance," but only by the supernatural work of the Holy

Spirit! All we need to do is *believe* by faith and obey the Holy Spirit, and then we will receive the blessing! As we have seen in scripture, spiritual transformation is not born out of effort or performance, but out of faith, obedience, and trust in the Lord's promises, believing that God is faithful and that He will do it!

Unforgiveness Can Block the Gift!

As we choose to receive God's forgiveness and forgive ourselves and others, we will be able to live out the empowerment of the giftings of the Holy Spirit! In ministry, I have seen that some people desire the baptism of the Holy Spirit, but because they hold a root of unforgiveness and bitterness toward God and others and even themselves, they cannot experience a deeper revelation of the Holy Spirit through receiving the baptism of the Holy Spirit. Why? Because unforgiveness blocks the gift. It is imperative that we choose to obey the Father as Jesus did and release all unforgiveness in our hearts. If we choose not to forgive, we will be choosing the path of offence, which grieves the Holy Spirit. In fact, in scripture Jesus said, "woe unto him, through whom [the offences] come" (Luke 17:1). Choosing to hold a grudge while withholding forgiveness from someone is the same thing as becoming offended. If we allow a root of bitterness and offence to enter our minds, our ability to hear the voice of God can become distorted or minimized. Think of an old radio dial. If you can't dial into the station you want to listen to, you will hear static noise, making it difficult to hear what the person on the radio is saying. It's the same with the Holy Spirit. You won't be able to tune into the place in the spirit where you can hear God's voice if your mind and heart are full of spiritual "static" from unforgiveness, bitterness, anger, malice, or retaliation. Please realize that when we do not choose to forgive as Jesus did, we may not be able to be receive from the Holy Spirit, because unforgiveness grieves the Holy Spirit.

To See the Kingdom of God

Once again, unless we are born again as Jesus taught, we will not "see" the kingdom of God.

Let's look again at two verses in John.

> Except a man be born again [or "from above"], he cannot see the kingdom of God. (John 3:3)

> Which were born, not of blood, nor of the will of the flesh, nor of the will of man, but of God. (John 1:13)

Notice the word "see" in John 3:3: if you are not born again, you will not "see" the Kingdom of God. According to *Strong's Concordance*, the word "see" in Greek is *"horaō,"* which means "To see with the eyes, to see with the mind, to perceive or know, to become acquainted with by experience, to experience, to show."[67]

The Word of God instructs us that if we want to see, perceive, and understand the deeper things, the mysteries of God, and the Kingdom of Heaven, we must allow the Holy Spirit to baptize us with His fire and be "born again" of the Spirit (Luke 3:16). Hallelujah! There is no condemnation, but rather only a beautiful invitation to come and receive the mysteries of God that are available to you through the power of the Holy Spirit.

Will you pray this prayer with me?

> Father, I want to have a heart that is open and able to receive all that you have for me. I repent of all unbelief, and I choose to receive Your Holy Spirit baptism. Father, I want to see the Kingdom. Help me to obey your Word and allow the Holy Spirit to flow in and through me so I can become all You made me to be. I give You permission to baptize me in the Holy Spirit, in Jesus's name. Amen.

---

[67] James Strong, *Strong's Exhaustive Concordance of the Bible* (Nashville, Tennessee: Abingdon Press, 1986), Strong's G3708.

TEN

Do You Know Me?

Not everyone that saith unto me, Lord, Lord, shall enter into the kingdom of heaven; but he that doeth the will of my Father which is in heaven. Many will say to me in that day, Lord, Lord, have we not prophesied in thy name? and in thy name have cast out devils? and in thy name done many wonderful works? And then will I profess unto them, I never knew you: depart from me, ye that work iniquity.
—Matthew 7:21–23

In January 2020, the Holy Spirit began to speak these verses to me, which led to weeks of praying and seeking the Lord about a verse that I could not ignore. The passage in Matthew 7:21–3 began to weigh heavily on my heart as I wondered, "What exactly is Jesus saying here?" After seeking the Lord, I believe these verses reveal that good works— even the performing of miracles, signs, and wonders—cannot produce true faith or make us justified before God; nor can they qualify us for heaven! Instead we must have a revelation of Jesus Christ through faith and a by the power of the Holy Spirit. In other words, spiritual maturity and character are not proven by the demonstration of spiritual gifts or miracles, but rather through a heart encounter with Jesus, resulting in a transformed heart and a *changed life*. From this place of true encounter with God (Father, Son, and Holy Spirit), we begin to die to self (selfish ambitions, fleshly desires, and anything that is contrary to the will of God) and live to give God glory!

I think it is interesting to notice the part of the verse in which professed believers of Jesus claim they prophesied, cast out devils, and did many wonderful *works* in the name of Jesus, and yet Jesus still says to them, "I never knew you: depart from me, ye that work iniquity." How can this be? The trouble is that good works will not produce relationship. However, God, who is faithful, will always honor His word as well as true faith. The issue is not whether people are experiencing miracles, healing, and the like. This issue is that when it comes to salvation and entering heaven, none of those good works, even when they are done in the name of Jesus, will get you there. Only a relationship with Jesus Christ by faith through His grace and the infilling of the Holy Spirit will.

Spiritual Gifts Will Not Produce Spiritual Character

Allow me to elaborate on this concept for a moment. Scripture states that "the gifts and calling of God are irrevocable" and "without repentance," (Romans 11:29 NASB and KJV). This means that receiving spiritual gifts and abilities from God does not equate to spiritual maturity or character and certainly does not "qualify" us before God, either. Additionally, if our spiritual gifts are given to us from God and are never taken from us, that would mean they cannot be contingent upon our behavior, religious beliefs, or rituals. Therefore, we can rightly determine that spiritual giftings cannot and *do not* equate righteousness or sincere faith in Jesus Christ.

I have learned the hard way that spiritual character is not a result of our spiritual gifts. Rather, spiritual character is a direct result of *relationship with Jesus*. It is so important that we resist becoming enamored with or idolizing believers who are "gifted" spiritually, assuming that their gifts are proof of spiritual maturity or character. Additionally, we must guard against valuing our spiritual gifts over Biblical knowledge of Jesus Christ, so that we do not become preoccupied with ourselves and others rather than being fully devoted to Jesus. This form of idolatry is a result of the sin of pride and can lead to a future spiritual fall. It is imperative to understand that gifts do not equate character, so that we will avoid becoming arrogant and prideful as a result of our spiritual gifts. Knowing this, we can now understand how these professed believers of Jesus addressed in Matthew 7:21–3 could assume that they would be permitted to enter heaven based upon their spiritual giftings and their performance rather than upon their relationship with Jesus Christ as a result of real, sincere, surrendered faith in Him.

Remember: Jesus said the words "I never knew you" to people who considered themselves His followers! This is a humbling and sobering reminder to each of us to keep our eyes fully on Jesus rather than on ourselves, our abilities, and our spiritual gifts! Do you remember the words of Jesus to the disciples after they returned from ministering for the first time without Jesus present with them? They returned ignited and overjoyed at all they were able to do in the Spirit and performed miracles, signs and wonders: "Behold, I give unto you the authority to trample on serpents and scorpions, and over all the power of the enemy: and nothing shall by any means hurt you. Notwithstanding in this rejoice not, that the spirits are subject unto you; but rather rejoice, because your names are written in heaven" (Luke 10:19–20).

Don't miss this! Rather than celebrating all the disciples had done in *His* name, Jesus reminded them of the greatest gift of all: that their "names are written in heaven"—meaning they will have eternal life. Here Jesus is presenting a strong statement that religious works—even supernatural, powerful, miraculous works—cannot and do not produce salvation and eternal life.

"Their Heart Is Far From Me"

This story draws my mind to a verse where Jesus said that some people may profess to know and love Him, but their *hearts* are *far* from Him: "This people draweth nigh unto me with their mouth, and honoureth me with their lips; but their heart is far from me" (Matthew 15:8).

Have we not seen this mindset emerging in our culture today? In Matthew 24, Jesus warns of the signs of the end times. I believe, without a doubt, that we are living in an end-time hour, as we are beginning to witness end-time events unfolding more and more by the day. Just as in the days of Jeremiah, in the days preceding the exile of God's people out of Israel into captivity in Babylon, false prophets, false prophetic words, and rebellion are running rampant. We must consider the reality that many believers may not fully understand what it means to truly love God, because they do not have a personal relationship with Jesus Christ through faith and have not been sealed to Him by the power of the Holy Spirit and therefore do not know the real Jesus.

Jesus warns us that the enemy himself, who is Satan, will appear as "an angel of light" (2 Corinthians 11:14), offering a cheap counterfeit for what only God can do. This is why we must beware of false prophets, who will appear at first as harmless as sheep but inwardly are ravening wolves. Now more than ever, we must pray for spiritual discernment and wisdom to recognize what is really of God and to avoid the counterfeit. The good news is that we can know the difference by knowing the Word of God and by examining the fruit of a person or ministry: "Beware of false prophets, which come to you in sheep's clothing, but inwardly they are ravening wolves. Ye shall know them by their fruits. Do men gather grapes of thorns, or figs of thistles? Even so every good tree bringeth forth good fruit; but a corrupt tree bringeth forth evil fruit. A good tree cannot bring forth evil fruit, neither can a corrupt tree bring forth good fruit. Every tree that bringeth not forth good fruit is hewn down, and cast into the fire. Wherefore by their fruits ye shall know them" (Matthew 7:15–20).

Galatians 5 clarifies what kind of "fruit" Jesus is speaking of here, and how it is starkly different from the works of the flesh:

> Now the works of the flesh are manifest, which are these; Adultery, fornication, uncleanness, lasciviousness, Idolatry, witchcraft, hatred, variance, emulations, wrath, strife, seditions, heresies, Envyings, murders, drunkenness, revellings, and such like: of the which I tell you before, as I have also told you in time past, that they which do such things shall not inherit the kingdom of God. But the fruit of the Spirit is love, joy, peace, longsuffering, gentleness, goodness, faith, Meekness, temperance: against such there is no law. And they that are Christ's have crucified the flesh with the affections

and lusts. If we live in the Spirit, let us also walk in the Spirit. (Galatians 5:19–25)

You Will Know Them by Their Fruit

If you want to be able to determine whether a miracle or manifestation is truly from the Holy Spirit, look at the fruit! Does this fruit produce love, joy, unity, and peace in the Lord? Does it align with God's patience and gentleness? Does it encourage faith and faithfulness and produce kindness, forbearance, longsuffering, and self- control? Or does it result in envy and vainglory, producing lasciviousness, hatred, and abuse?

Apply this biblical discernment to the fruit of any minister or doctrine, and you will be able to weed out cults and abusive so-called ministers. When you are evaluating the fruit, remember to observe the following : (1) Is there corruption, envy, jealously or strife? (2) Is there sexual immorality? (3) Is there a spirit of wrath or rage? (4) Is there a lust for money, power, and influence? If the answer to any of those questions is yes, it is time to move on. I urge you to strongly consider disassociating from anyone operating in what looks like the power of God but who then lives a life of hypocrisy, abandoning the sacred and holy teachings of the scriptures:

> If there arise among you a prophet, or a dreamer of dreams, and giveth thee a sign or a wonder, And the sign or the wonder come to pass, whereof he spake unto thee, saying, Let us go after other gods, which thou hast not known, and let us serve them; Thou shalt not hearken unto the words of that prophet, or that dreamer of dreams: for the Lord your God proveth you, to know whether ye love the Lord your God with all your heart and with all your soul. Ye shall walk after the Lord your God, and fear him, and keep his commandments, and obey his voice, and ye shall serve him, and cleave unto him. (Deuteronomy 13:1–4)

The mark of a true minister of God is that he or she will know Jesus through the Holy Spirit, abide in God's Spirit, and minister by His Spirit. Only then will we minister with the fruit of His Spirit evident in our lives! True servants of Jesus Christ are willing to choose to "die to self," abandon selfish desires, ambitions, and pride, and give Jesus all the glory, for He alone is worthy! The heart of the matter is this: if we love God, we will lay down our lives for the sheep—which is exactly what Jesus did! He alone is worthy of all glory and honor because He went to the cross, died, and rose again on the third day, obeying the Father, and He is now "high and lifted up" in heaven! Jesus Christ alone is the worthy Lamb of God: "Worthy is the Lamb that was slain to receive power, and riches, and wisdom, and strength, and honor, and glory, and blessing" (Revelation 5:12).

Guard Your Heart

As we consider what we have learned from scripture, some of you may be asking, "How can we, as believers, protect our pure faith and prevent drifting away from Jesus and his truth?" The answer is that we must guard our hearts by renewing our minds in the Word of God and develop intimacy with Jesus from the secret place of prayer and worship as we enjoy His presence. From this holy place of real relationship, we hear the voice of God through the Holy Spirit, who will witness the truth to our hearts: "But when the Comforter is come, whom I will send unto you from the Father, even the Spirit of truth, which proceedeth from the Father, he shall testify of me: And ye also shall bear witness, because ye have been with me from the beginning" (John 15:26–7).

As we daily immerse ourselves in God's Word, we will wrap God's Word around our life experience, be empowered to avoid unwanted spiritual warfare, and cast down every lie of the enemy! "(For the weapons of our warfare are not carnal, but mighty through God to the pulling down of strong holds;)[68] Casting down imaginations, and every high thing that exalteth itself against the knowledge of God, and

---

[68] See Eph. 3:16: "That he would grant you, according to the riches of his glory, to be strengthened with might by his Spirit in the inner man . . ."

bringing into captivity every thought to the obedience of Christ …"[69] (2 Corinthians 10:4–5).

As we obey God's Word, our confidence will grow as we see His faithfulness throughout scripture *and* in His sovereign care over our lives. The result is a life full of joy and a vibrant, surrendered relationship with Jesus Christ! The good news is that when we totally rely upon Him for our every need, desire, and purpose, we enter a relationship of trust in God, believing He is faithful and true to His word, and we will avoid spiritual deception, self-idolatry, and unbelief. As we choose to connect to the vine, who is Jesus Christ, He will enable us to operate in His pure anointing that flows from relationship with Him and by the power of the Holy Spirit whom He sent:

> I am the true vine, and my Father is the husbandman. Every branch in me that beareth not fruit he taketh away: and every branch that beareth fruit, he purgeth it, that it may bring forth more fruit. Now ye are clean through the word which I have spoken unto you. Abide in me, and I in you. As the branch cannot bear fruit of itself, except it abide in the vine; no more can ye, except ye abide in me. I am the vine, ye are the branches: He that abideth in me, and I in him, the same bringeth forth much fruit: for without me ye can do nothing. If a man abide not in me, he is cast forth as a branch, and is withered; and men gather them, and cast them into the fire, and they are burned. If ye abide in me, and my words abide in you, ye shall ask what ye will, and it shall be done unto you. (John 15:1–7)

If we truly love Jesus and want to follow Him, we will stay connected to Him through His Word, prayer, worship, and lifestyle. Then, as we continue to be obedient to God's Word, the Holy Spirit will confirm the Word in our hearts, resulting in a revival igniting our hearts as we

---

[69]   See 1 Cor. 1:19: "For it is written, I will destroy the wisdom of the wise, and will bring to nothing the understanding of the prudent."

fall more and more in love with Jesus through an intimate relationship with him.

Pray with me:

> Father, I want to know Your Son, Jesus Christ, and to be known by Him. Please help me to reject the world and chose to follow you so that nothing will stand between us. I repent for any counterfeit religion in my life and choose today to step out in faith embracing a vibrant, intimate, and powerful relationship with you through following Jesus Christ. Help me to die to self and live for Christ that I may glorify Him in all that I do and say, for Your glory, in Jesus's name. Amen.

ELEVEN

I Came to Do the Will of My Father

> Not everyone that saith unto me, Lord, Lord, shall
> enter into the kingdom of heaven; but he that doeth
> the will of my Father which is in heaven.
> —Matthew 7:21

Does this verse of scripture line up with what we learned about salvation by faith and relationship with Jesus? We know we can't earn God's love; only our pure faith can bring us into a divine place of favor and freedom in Christ through surrendering our lives to Him. So why would God tell us in His Word that unless we do His *will*, we cannot enter the Kingdom of Heaven? Doesn't that sound "works based"? Yes, it does. But I believe that what God is saying here does not have to do with actions, or "doing," but rather points us to go deeper in the revelation of God's Word to understand what it means to *do* God's will.

Let's look at what Jesus says about this in scripture: "For I came down from heaven, not to do mine own will, but the will of him that sent me"[70] (John 6:38).

Once again, we see in scripture that we must have a personal, intimate relationship with Jesus. Only then will we truly have "the mind of Christ" (1 Corinthians 2:16). Without the mind of Christ, it will be impossible to obey the Father and do *His* will. What exactly does it mean to have the mind of Christ? It means to *know* Him, *love* Him, and

---

[70] See John 4:34: "Jesus saith unto them, My meat is to do the will of him that sent me, and to finish his work."

do His will. As we engage in a personal relationship with Jesus by the help of the Holy Spirit, He will confirm the Word (who is Jesus) to our hearts! Once we enter a real relationship with Jesus Christ, we are sealed by the Holy Spirit by faith (Ephesians 1:13; Titus 3:4–7) and washed by the blood of Jesus—His blood that flowed from His body while He was hanging on the cross. When you are sealed by the Holy Spirit through faith in Jesus, His blood becomes a covering of protection over your life. This is reason to rejoice, knowing that when we belong to Jesus, we will have power to overcome condemnation, shame, fear, and regret! "There is therefore now no condemnation to them which are in Christ Jesus, who walk not after the flesh, but after the Spirit. For the law of the Spirit of life in Christ Jesus hath made me free from the law of sin and death" (Romans 8: 1–2).

It is from this place of redemption and freedom that we can trust Jesus and His finished work on the cross and begin to understand just how expansive and far-reaching His love truly is! Paul said it this way: "For I am persuaded, that neither death, nor life, nor angels, nor principalities, nor powers, nor things present, nor things to come, Nor height, nor depth, nor any other creature, shall be able to separate us from the love of God, which is in Christ Jesus our Lord" (Romans 8:38–9).

Now *that* is what I call *good news!* After suffering so much condemnation and fear from cult religion, and then receiving a revelation of my true identify in Christ, I have come to understand that, truly, nothing you or I have done in the past that we have repented of can separate us from the love of Jesus Christ! Additionally, we are now declared justified and holy before God in love! "According as he hath chosen us in him before the foundation of the world, that we should be holy and without blame before him in love ..." (Ephesians 1:4).

I don't know about you, but I think it is amazing what this scripture reveals about our identity in Christ. Whether we fully understand how or why is not important. Rather, let's focus on choosing to believe what the Word of God says—that we were chosen by God, before the world was created, to become holy and without blame or condemnation so that we could one day stand before him in love. Imagine it: standing before Jesus after this life, enveloped and surrounded in and by His love. Hallelujah! Just the thought of it makes me weep. Jesus is so *wonderful!* This is the joy of being "born again" as children of God and lovers of Jesus. This is why we will *want* to obey the Father—because just like Jesus, we will be filled with such gratitude and love for Him that we can't help but live to love Him, worship Him, and adore Him. Interestingly, this is how we please Him through our genuine worship and love!

Falling In Love With Jesus!

Truly, as we choose to worship and adore Jesus, we will love Him more and more each day! From this place of obedience (choosing to believe in Him by faith), our devotion to Jesus will increase to the point at which our lives can't help but give Him glory. What about you? Do you want to love Jesus with all your heart? I can personally testify that when we choose to follow Jesus by faith, we can begin a relationship with Him that is intimate, surrendered, authentic, and unadulterated. We can be "true worshippers" who have life-giving relationships with Jesus (see John 4:23–4). This is how we become true bridal "lovers" of Jesus and will not only obey Him but are also willing to lay down our very *lives* for Him! As we surrender our will and do *His* will, and as we allow the Holy Spirit to reveal the pure love of Jesus to our hearts, our relationships with Jesus will begin to deepen and flourish. From this place of overflow, we will be able to truly have the mind of Christ, and it will become easy to do the will of the Father. It is only when we believe what Jesus did for us—and receive a revelation of His great grace, forgiveness, and love even when we don't deserve it—that we will be able to truly do the will of Father and obey Him. Remember: the word "obedience" in the Greek means "belief." The more we know and love Jesus, the more we will be able to believe in Him and what He said. From that place of knowing and being known by Jesus will flow gratitude—not from obligation or a "have to" mentality, but from a genuine place of trust and desire to obey Jesus because we *love Him.*

I can testify to you that as we renew our minds daily in the Word of God—through reading the Bible, prayer, and worship,—Jesus will become more real and personal in ways we can't even imagine. I like to call this place of surrender "falling in love with Jesus," because the more I renew my mind in the Word of God and worship Jesus, the more I *love* Jesus! Think about it: any time we enter a new relationship with someone, we want to spend more time with them and get to know them better, don't we? So it is with knowing and loving Jesus! Once we encounter His love, we find ourselves wanting to know Him more and more. As time goes on, we will even begin to crave time with Him and won't be able to survive our mundane lives without Him! Scripture says, "Draw near to God and He will draw near to you" (James 4:8 NKJV). In Jeremiah 29:12–13, we read, "Then shall ye call upon me, and ye shall go and pray unto me, and I will hearken unto you. And ye shall seek me, and find me, when ye shall search for me with all your heart." From the place of intimacy, the anointing and power of God will flow like a river of life, refreshing our spirits. It will no longer be difficult to live for God and do His will, because just like Jesus, we will be empowered by the Spirit to obey God because we love Him and are loved by Him!

Worship and the Word!

I have discovered that in worshipping Jesus Christ, I can become totally lost in a deep, joyful, transforming place in the spirit where I can experience His deep love for me. I like to call this place in the spirit "throne room worship." This is where the anointing and presence of God lives. From this powerful place in the presence of Jesus, we can experience His love for us so powerfully that even strongholds (unwanted beliefs, patterns, and habits) are destroyed and removed, setting us free from sin, shame, fear, condemnation, and destructive habits in our lives! Do you want to be set free? *Worship Him!* Do you want to be a powerful force in the Kingdom of God? *Worship Him!* Do you want to pray with authority? *Worship Him!* Do you want to see a breakthrough in your life? *Worship Him!* Joyful, surrendered worship of our King Jesus is the most powerful way to commune with Him and be transformed by His love! When we worship Him, we are allowing the Word of God to penetrate our hearts, going down deeply to the "innermost parts": the deepest parts of our spiritual beings. In this way, we can powerfully experience the Word of God, hiding the Word in our hearts. (See Psalm 119:11.) I have been blessed to minister to the Lord Jesus Christ in worship since I was twelve years old, when I began to sing for Jesus. I have seen how worship opens the window of heaven and allows the light of Jesus in. Some of my most powerful visions and encounters with Jesus have occurred while I have been blessed to enter heavenly realms of the Spirit through worshipping Him.

When we worship Jesus and soak in the Word of God, we allow His presence to saturate our hearts and minds with His glorious light. As we do this, we will have powerful, fresh encounters with the love of Jesus! Once we have surrendered everything (our hearts, desires, and personal ambitions) to Jesus, it is important that we know how to *stay* in that place of surrender and trust. Worship is your relationship maintenance plan! Choosing to actively worship Jesus is a powerful way to maintain a deep and intimate relationship with Jesus. Additionally, the Word of God is the revelation of Jesus Christ, and feasting on His words will protect us from deception from the enemy and from the culture of the world we are living in (Romans 12:2; 2 Timothy 3:16). As we feast on His Word and allow the Holy Spirit to flow in and through us, we will be able to encounter the love of Jesus and resist the devil and his evil schemes. We will also be better equipped to rebuke the enemy and command him to flee from us (James 4:7). Choosing to submit our lives to the lordship of Jesus Christ and follow Him in obedience is the key. One thing is for sure: the enemy wants to steal, kill, and destroy your faith (John 10:10). But remember what Jesus said to Simon Peter in Luke 22:32: "But I have prayed for thee, that thy faith fail not."

Now rest in the words Jesus speaks in John 6:39: "And this is the Father's will which hath sent me, that of all which he hath given me I should lose nothing, but should raise it up again at the last day."

Victory comes into the life of a believer of Jesus Christ when he or she chooses to believe the Word of God. One of the most powerful passages of Scripture we have in our "arsenal" of spiritual weaponry to fight against the enemy's attacks on our pure faith is found in Titus 3:3–7: "For we ourselves also were sometimes foolish, disobedient, deceived, serving divers lusts and pleasures, living in malice and envy, hateful, and hating one another. But after that the kindness and love of God our Saviour toward man appeared, not by works of righteousness which we have done, but according to his mercy he saved us, by the washing of regeneration, and renewing of the Holy Ghost; Which he shed on us abundantly through Jesus Christ our Saviour; That being justified by his grace, we should be made heirs according to the hope of eternal life."

Remember: Faith Is the Work!

I want to testify to you that as a born-again Christian, you are safely held in the arms of Jesus! We need to push back against the attacks of the enemy; we need to stay in a place of surrendered obedience to God's will. James said it this way: "Faith without works is dead" (James 2:20 NKJV). Good works are the result of true faith in Jesus Christ. We have seen in scripture that only our faith, which produces good works, will please God. So why does God tell us to do His will? Because He knows that when we obey His will, we truly love Him and not ourselves! We can see several examples in scripture of God's people being delivered and set free, and then, one step at a time, they choose to return to self-idolatry and the worship of false gods. How sad! So, what keeps us from doing the same thing? *Relationship with Jesus Christ.* When we love someone, we desire to please them and serve them, and our lives display that desire. When we know Jesus and love Him as He has loved us, we will be willing to lose everything for Him, die to self, and receive the fullness of His blessings in our lives, and we will overcome the evil one!

Pray with me:

Father, I want to do your will! I choose to worship Jesus Christ alone! I humbly ask for a deeper revelation of Jesus so I can experience a more powerful, chain-breaking, life-changing, victorious relationship with Him! Thank you for sending your Holy Spirit to confirm and reveal more of Jesus Christ and his love for me! In Jesus's name, Amen.

TWELVE

Prophecy, Dreams, and Visions

And it shall come to pass afterward, that I will pour out my
spirit upon all flesh; and your sons and your daughters shall
prophesy, your old men shall dream dreams, your young
men shall see visions: And also upon the servants and upon
the handmaids in those days will I pour out my spirit.
—Joel 2:28–9

Over the years, many have wondered, "Are dreams, visions, and
prophecies like those we see in the Bible still occurring today? Can
believers have dreams and visions or receive words of prophecy today?"
I am delighted to answer with a resounding yes! Over the years, the Holy
Spirit has given me numerous dreams and visions that have only expanded
my understanding of scripture and the heart of Jesus. Additionally, the
Holy Spirit will give revelation knowledge to us to encourage, exhort,
and edify us as individual believers and as the body of Christ as a whole.

The Word of God tells us that believers, men and women alike, can
enjoy a deep, intimate relationship with Jesus Christ equally and are
both able to receive and operate in the gifts of the Holy Spirit. In Joel
2:28–29, we read about the prophecy that in the end times, the Holy
Spirit will be poured out in the last days, birthing the prophetic ministry,
resulting in miracles, signs, and wonders. In Acts 2, the fulfillment of
this prophecy began when the Holy Spirit fell upon the twelve apostles
at Pentecost in the appearance of cloven flames of fire over their heads.

Additionally, the Holy Spirit is continually poured out onto believers
in the book of Acts, which cites that even women prophesied under

the unction of the Holy Spirit (Acts 21:9). Isn't it wonderful to see in scripture how the Holy Spirit will come upon the sons and daughters of God and is not gender exclusive? We also see clearly that the power of the Holy Spirit is not limited to only a select few anointed ministers but is freely given to all the body of Christ! Through the power of the Holy Spirit, every believer can receive revelation from God. The Holy Spirit enables us to operate in the same resurrection power that Jesus Christ imparted to the first apostles. (Romans 1:1–6, Philippians 3:10)

> But ye have an unction from the Holy One, and ye know all things. (1 John 2:20)[71]

> But the anointing which ye have received of him abideth in you, and ye need not that any man teach you: but as the same anointing teacheth you of all things, and is truth, and is no lie, and even as it hath taught you, ye shall abide in him. (1 John 2:27)

> Now he which [establishes] us with you in Christ, and hath anointed us, is God ... (2 Corinthians 1:21)

> Jesus Himself, after his forty-day fast in the wilderness, announced from Scripture that the Spirit of the Lord God was upon Him and had anointed Him.

> The Spirit of the Lord GOD is upon me; because the LORD hath anointed me to preach good tidings unto the meek; he hath sent me to bind up the brokenhearted, to proclaim liberty to the captives, and the opening of the prison to them that are bound[72] ... To appoint unto them

---

[71] See Heb. 1:9: "Thou hast loved righteousness, and hated iniquity; therefore God, *even* thy God, hath anointed thee with the oil of gladness above thy fellows."

[72] See Matthew 3:17: "And lo a voice from heaven, saying, This is my beloved Son, in whom I am well pleased." See also Matthew 11:5: "The blind receive their sight, and the lame walk, the lepers are cleansed, and the deaf hear, the dead are raised up, and the poor have the gospel preached to them." See also Psalm 147:3: "He healeth the broken in heart, and bindeth up their wounds."

that mourn in Zion, to give unto them beauty for ashes, the oil of joy for mourning, the garment of praise for the spirit of heaviness; that they might be called trees of righteousness, the planting of the LORD, that he might be glorified. (Isaiah 61:1, 3)

Here we see Jesus demonstrating to us how the anointing "comes upon us" so we can operate under His power and authority on earth by moving in signs and wonders today! Do you desire to see the miraculous occur today? Embrace the truth that the Holy Spirit has been poured out and is here now and available to you. All you need to do is receive Him! We can discern, or "hear," the voice of God collectively through a knowledge of scripture as well as from the Holy Spirit. Remember: Jesus wants to heal you and set you free! He loves to reveal His heart and love for you through prophetic dreams and visions, through His word, and through worship and prayer. Jesus has made a way for us to experience Him through revelation by the Holy Spirit so that we may know without a doubt that we are never alone. Jesus never has and never will fail us, and He reminds us of this truth:

I will not leave you comfortless, I will come to you. (John 14:18)

He healeth the broken in heart, and bindeth up their wounds. (Psalm 147:3)[73]

As I have committed myself to reading the Word of God, praying, worshipping at the feet of Jesus, and encountering His love, I have

---

[73] See Psalm 51:17: "The sacrifices of God *are* a broken spirit: a broken and a contrite heart, O God, thou wilt not despise." See also Isaiah 61:1: "The Spirit of the Lord GOD *is* upon me; because the LORD hath anointed me to preach good tidings unto the meek; he hath sent me to bind up the brokenhearted, to proclaim liberty to the captives, and the opening of the prison to *them that are* bound." See also Luke 4:18: "The Spirit of the Lord *is* upon me, because he hath anointed me to preach the gospel to the poor; he hath sent me to heal the brokenhearted, to preach deliverance to the captives, and recovering of sight to the blind, to set at liberty them that are bruised."

experienced healing, peace, and unspeakable joy. Truly, Jesus has healed my broken heart. But how does Jesus do that? How does He heal our broken hearts? The answer is simple: His love is "shed abroad in our hearts" (Romans 5:5) by the power of the Holy Spirit. What a privilege it is to enter the presence of Jesus, who is one with the Father and the Holy Spirit.

I Am Not Ashamed of the Gospel!

As I have chosen to keep my eyes on Jesus, regardless of the criticism or spiritual warfare going on around me, I have been able to break through this natural realm into the realm of the spirit and straight to the heart of Jesus through visions and dreams as I have been in prayer and worship. I don't know where I would be without encountering the heart of God through the prophetic ministry of Jesus. I am not ashamed of the prophetic ministry and the power and victory we can take hold of when we believe in faith that God still speaks to His people through prophecy, dreams, and visions that are in agreement with the gospel of Jesus Christ and His Word. Powerful breakthroughs in my spiritual life have come as I have received from the Lord through the prophetic anointing. These encounters with the Holy Spirit have encouraged me and helped me to mature in my faith. As a result, my spiritual life has deepened as new revelations have come forth, revealing more and more of the heart of God and His love! "And hope maketh not ashamed; because the love of God is shed abroad in our hearts by the Holy Ghost which is given unto us." (Romans 5:5)

It is from these encounters with the Holy Spirit that I draw vision, purpose, and plans for the ministry, as well as revelation of my own identity in Christ. Many times, the direction I have received from the Lord has given me the courage to face many storms and challenges. On occasion, the Spirit of the Lord has visited me in dreams and visions to guard my heart before difficult days ahead. In some instances, these very encounters with the Lord protected my heart and preserved my faith. This is another reason why we need the pure prophetic ministry overflowing from our time spent in the presence of Jesus—so that we can receive fresh faith and strength to face what is ahead. Scripture reminds us that this life is full of warfare that is not only fought in the natural but also in the spiritual realm: "For we wrestle not against flesh and blood, but against principalities, against powers, against the rulers of the darkness of this world, against spiritual wickedness in high places" (Ephesians 6:12).

We are not just facing trouble in the world we live in, or the "natural realm"—what we can see with our eyes and experience with our flesh. We also face challenges, or "warfare," in the "spirit realm"—the realm of Spirit, which we cannot see with our natural eyes but only with our spiritual eyes. We need to know how to discern in the spiritual realm what is happening in the natural realm.

The Holy Spirit enables us to "see" or understand spiritual truths and awakens our spiritual gifts, given to us by the Lord Himself. These gifts of the spirit are available to every believer (see 1 Corinthians 12). The prophetic ministry operates by the direction of the Holy Spirit and is available to every believer. As we open our hearts to receiving the Holy Spirit through faith in Jesus and receiving the Holy Spirit's power "upon us," as described in Acts 2 and 9 and John 3 and 4, the gifts of the Spirit are awakened and enhanced, enabling believers of Christ to stand on His Word and fight against the powers of darkness. From this place of power and equipping of the Holy Spirit, we will be able to stand in victory over every evil plot of the enemy! How good is our faithful God to equip us with every spiritual gift we need to overcome the evil in this world? The finished work of Jesus on the cross and the sending of the Holy Spirit, who is the "promise of the Father" (Acts 1:4–9), makes all things possible! Truly we have everything we need to live powerful lives and walk in victory in Christ!

Another Gospel?

One word of caution is to always be sure that what you claim to see or hear in the form of prophetic visions and dreams must *always* agree with the Word of God! The apostle Paul warned us of the danger that can come from receiving "another gospel" through deception: "But though we, or an angel from heaven, preach any other gospel unto you than that which we have preached unto you, let him be accursed.[74] As we said before, so say I now again, If any man preach any other gospel unto you than that ye have received, let him be accursed"[75] (Galatians 1:8–9).

As I have continually chosen to seek the Lord daily in the secret place, encountering Jesus and the heart of God through the power of the Holy Spirit, my faith has grown exponentially—and so can yours! Looking back, I realize that the Holy Spirit continues to reveal the love of Jesus to me day after day as I spend time tuning my spiritual ears to hear His voice in prayer, worship, praise, journaling, and studying His Word. Twelve years ago, as I began to develop this daily discipline, Jesus began to reveal Himself to me more and more! Now I simply cannot tolerate life without daily encounters with Him. This is such a beautiful walk with Jesus that I now enjoy, and I encourage you to believe that you can enjoy it too.

In 2014, I began to make a practice of writing down what the Lord was speaking through the Holy Spirit. The Word of God tells us to "write the vision, and make it plain" so the people can "run" (see Habakkuk 2:2). It is important that we share what we hear from the Lord, because those very revelations, as they agree with the Word of God, can help encourage people to continue in faith and be encouraged in their own lives. We must even share prophetic warnings, if received through the Holy Spirit and confirmed through the Word of God, for the purpose of protecting the people of God.

Do Not Despise Prophecy

Scripture specifically warns us not to despise prophecy (1 Thessalonians 5:20) or quench the Holy Spirit (1 Thessalonians 5:19). We should not be afraid to share what we see and hear from the Lord and should have the freedom to be a blessing to the body of Christ as we exhort, encourage, and warn other believers when needed and as

---

[74] See 1 Corinthians 16:22: "If any man love not the Lord Jesus Christ, let him be Anathema Maranatha."

[75] See Deuteronomy 4:2: "Ye shall not add unto the word which I command you, neither shall ye diminish *ought* from it, that ye may keep the commandments of the LORD your God which I command you."

the Holy Spirit directs. A favorite verse of mine, 2 Corinthians 3:17, reads, "Now the Lord is that Spirit: and where the Spirit of the Lord is, there is liberty." As the Word of God declares, we should not despise prophecy but should follow the biblical model, which is to test every spirit to see whether it is of God (1 John 4:1–6). Additionally, when we receive a prophetic word, we should wait for confirmation from two or more witnesses to ensure that what we are seeing and hearing is both biblical and of the Lord (2 Corinthians 13:1).

Yes, there can be false prophets and lying spirits, and the devil can masquerade or disguise himself as an angel of light, so we must be careful to train ourselves how to discern the difference between something that is from God and something that is not. First of all, we must use common sense. The Word tells us that God does not give us a "spirit of fear; but of power, and of love, and of a sound mind" (2 Timothy 1:7). If we are experiencing a dream, vision, or prophetic word that causes us to fear, doubt, have anxiety, or oppose God's Word in any way, it is *not* from God! Scripture explains prophecy this way in this verse from Revelation: "And I fell at [the angel's] feet to worship him. And he said unto me, See thou do it not: I am thy fellow servant, and of thy brethren that have the testimony of Jesus: worship God: for the testimony of Jesus is the spirit of prophecy" (Revelation 19:10).

When we receive a prophetic dream, vision, or word from the Lord, we should be filled with peace, comfort, and joy. We can also receive warnings from the Holy Spirit, but the key is to watch out and guard against anyone or anything that attempts to cause shame, condemnation, or fear. The Holy Spirit does not operate that way, because godly correction is love and will be administered in a way that is loving (1 Timothy 5:1–2). Sadly, some ministers fall into the trap of what we call "ministering out of their flesh," in which they may claim to have had a vision, dream, or prophecy that does not confirm or agree with the Word of God. The good news is that a true prophetic word of the Lord will always produce the testimony of Jesus accompanied with the fruit of the Spirit: "But the fruit of the Spirit is love, joy, peace, longsuffering, gentleness, goodness, faith, Meekness, temperance: against such there is no law" (Galatians 5:22–3).

What a gift it is to experience the Holy Spirit speaking to us through the prophetic word, delivered and decreed from the mouth of anointed, mature believers who do not quench or silence the Holy Spirit! Remember what the Word of God says: "Quench not the Spirit. Despise not prophesyings" (1 Thessalonians 5:19–20). And there it is, plain and simple! Many people argue that we do not need prophetic words today because we have the Bible, which is full of prophecies of Jesus and examples of prophetic words: "The testimony of Jesus is the spirit of prophecy" (Revelation 19:10).

Additionally, we can hear directly from Jesus today by the unction of the Holy Spirit: "But ye have an unction from the Holy One, and ye know all things" (1 John 2:20).

Another powerful prophecy comes from the prophet Joel and was referenced by Peter regarding the pouring out of the Holy Spirit and the prophetic move of the Holy Spirit:

> But Peter, standing up with the eleven, lifted up his voice, and said unto them, Ye men of Judaea, and all ye that dwell at Jerusalem, be this known unto you, and hearken to my words: ... this is that which was spoken by the prophet Joel; And it shall come to pass in the last days, saith God, I will pour out of my Spirit upon all flesh: and your sons and your daughters shall prophesy, and your young men shall see visions, and your old men shall dream dreams. (Acts 2:14, 16–17)[76]

> And it shall come to pass afterward, that I will pour out my spirit upon all flesh; and your sons and your daughters shall prophesy, your old men shall dream dreams, your young men shall see visions: And also upon the servants and upon the handmaids in those days will I pour out my spirit. And I will shew wonders in the

---

[76]　See Acts 10:45: "And they of the circumcision which believed were astonished, as many as came with Peter, because that on the Gentiles also was poured out the gift of the Holy Ghost." See also Acts 21:9 "And the same man had four daughters, virgins, which did prophesy."

heavens and in the earth, blood, and fire, and pillars of smoke.[77] The sun shall be turned into darkness, and the moon into blood, before the great and terrible day of the LORD come.[78] And it shall come to pass, that whosoever shall call on the name of the LORD shall be delivered: for in mount Zion and in Jerusalem shall be deliverance, as the LORD hath said, and in the remnant[79] whom the LORD shall call. (Joel 2:28–32)

Notice the key themes from these verses:

- God will pour out His Spirit (Holy Spirit or Holy Ghost).
- Sons and daughters will prophesy.
- Old men will dream dreams.
- Young men will see visions.
- God will pour out his spirit upon the handmaids (women).
- There will be signs and wonders in the heavens and in the earth.
- Those who call on the name of the Lord will be delivered (saved).
- The remnant shall be called by the Lord.

Now, regarding the prophecy of Joel about the Holy Spirit being "poured out" in the last days, I ask you, do we not see this taking place in the church today? Do we not also see situations, ministries, and

---

[77] See Matthew 24:29: "Immediately after the tribulation of those days shall the sun be darkened, and the moon shall not give her light, and the stars shall fall from heaven, and the powers of the heavens shall be shaken." See also Acts 2:19: "And I will shew wonders in heaven above, and signs in the earth beneath; blood, and fire, and vapour of smoke."

[78] See Joel 3:15: "The sun and the moon shall be darkened, and the stars shall withdraw their shining."

[79] See Romans 10:13: "For whosoever shall call upon the name of the Lord shall be saved." See also Isaiah 11:11: "And it shall come to pass in that day, *that* the Lord shall set his hand again the second time to recover the remnant of his people, which shall be left, from Assyria, and from Egypt, and from Pathros, and from Cush, and from Elam, and from Shinar, and from Hamath, and from the islands of the sea." See also Romans 9:27: "Esaias also crieth concerning Israel, Though the number of the children of Israel be as the sand of the sea, a remnant shall be saved."

churches that do not allow the Holy Spirit to move freely among the believers? It is a sad thing to discover that in many cases, the Holy Spirit is being restrained or "quenched." Scripture says in 2 Corinthians 3:17 (NIV), "where the Spirit of the Lord is, there is freedom."

So, with all of scripture's instruction about the reality of the baptism of the Holy Spirit and about prophecy, dreams, and visions, why would so many believers reject this teaching? I think the root problem is unbelief (a lack of faith) and the fear of the unknown. If we do not spend time in the Word of God, in prayer, or in worship, our hearts can grow cold and callused. We need a touch from the Holy Spirit to help us encounter the supernatural power of God. If we never spend time in the Spirit encountering God, then it will naturally feel uncomfortable to do so in front of others in a more public setting like a church or even in a small Bible study. The truth is, as we open our hearts to God, He will pour out His love and power more and more. But God will not kick down the door of your heart. He wants to be invited.

Dreams and Visions

In the book of Genesis, we read about Joseph, who was sold into slavery in Egypt by his jealous brothers who hated him because he claimed to have received dreams and visions from God Himself. But later on, those very same brothers who hated Joseph were standing before him in Egypt, asking for provision and food during a great famine. There they stood in Pharaoh's court, bowing before Joseph, their younger brother, just as he had foretold! Joseph, who was now the right-hand man of Pharaoh himself, and ruling over all of Egypt, was in fact worthy of being honored and obeyed! This is an excellent example of how we must wait on the Lord for clarity about what He shows us! It may not make sense at first, but as we stay close to the Lord, He will reveal His plan for us over time. We can trust the Lord to comfort and protect us as He reveals His plans and purposes to us.

I have personally experienced this process of receiving a prophetic dream and not fully understanding what it meant at the time, but I trusted the Lord, and in time, He revealed the full meaning as I obeyed and believed in faith in what He had shown me.

In 2021, I was planning to embark on my first mission trip to Africa. In 2015, I had received a prophetic word that my feet would touch on many lands and that God was calling me to Africa. When the opportunity came six years later, I remembered the word and prayed. Simultaneously, I had been given a dream in which the Lord clearly showed me one word, "Ashanti," over the top of a geographical map. Immediately I woke up, alert and sharp. I asked the Lord, "What is that?" I then heard the voice of God say to me, "Look it up on your cell phone," and so I did. I was amazed to find that "Ashanti" is a region of Ghana in which the most powerful king of Ghana rules. Because the Lord gave me this dream, I decided to pursue sending my on-the-ground advisor in ministry in Ghana to visit the region and to report back. After seeking the Lord in prayer, I felt that I was to try to meet with the king of Ashanti in person to pray for him. My response was "Who am I, Lord?" Even though it all seemed rather outlandish, God gave me the faith to believe in what He wanted to do and to trust His perfect will. Radical obedience will always bring supernatural results! I was blessed to fly with my team to the Ashanti Kingdom in Kumasi, Ghana, and stand before the king in his court. This was unprecedented and led to my being allowed to meet with the king's staff and worship and pray with them. Hallelujah! I was also able to leave a copy of this book you are now reading for him, in hopes that when I return to Ghana he will receive the gospel of Jesus Christ. You see, it is not up to us to understand all that God is doing in the moment, but it is up to us to *obey* God. Then, when we are faithful in God's time and way, we will see the miracle. The following year, I was blessed to learn that Daniel Kolenda, head of Christ For All Nations ministry, held the largest crusade in their history resulting in 764,000 salvations. Believe it or not, CFAN's crusade was held in the very region God had sent me: Kumasi, Ghana!

The truth is, God *loves* doing outside-the-box, unusual, powerful things that will bring Him glory. Although it tested my own faith, Jesus gave me favor to believe for a supernatural move of God in Ghana because of what He had shown me in my dream. When we trust God and allow Him to reveal His mysteries to us, we will be able to soar high in the supernatural realm of the Spirit and do powerful Kingdom exploits for God's glory! In fact, Jesus revealed that we would do even greater things than we have seen Him do:

Verily, verily, I say unto you, He that believeth on me, the works that I do shall he do also; and greater works than these shall he do; because I go unto my Father. (John 14:12)

Jesus answered and said unto them, Verily I say unto you, If ye have faith, and doubt not, ye shall not only do this which is done to the fig tree, but also if ye shall say unto this mountain, Be thou removed, and be thou cast into the sea; it shall be done. (Matthew 21:21)[80]

And these signs shall follow them that believe; In my name shall they cast out devils; they shall speak with new tongues; They shall take up serpents; and if they drink any deadly thing, it shall not hurt them; they shall lay hands on the sick, and they shall recover. (Mark 16:17–8)[81]

Pray with me:

Father, I pray more believers will come to understand their true identity and authority in Christ, understanding that we are fully equipped by His grace and power, to operate in the pure anointing of the Holy Spirit and receive the prophetic ministry available to us as believers. Father, we ask you to use us for your glory. May we all become more effective and productive in producing powerful testimonies for the kingdom of God. In Jesus's name, Amen.

---

[80] See Matthew 17:20: "And Jesus said unto them, Because of your unbelief: for verily I say unto you, If ye have faith as a grain of mustard seed, ye shall say unto this mountain, Remove hence to yonder place; and it shall remove; and nothing shall be impossible unto you."

[81] See James 5:14: "Is any sick among you? let him call for the elders of the church; and let them pray over him, anointing him with oil in the name of the Lord."

THIRTEEN

Forgiveness Is Love

> Wherefore I say unto thee, Her sins, which are many, are forgiven; for she loved much: but to whom little is forgiven, the same loveth little.
> —Luke 7:47

J esus was clear when He said to us that if we do not forgive others of their trespasses, our Father in heaven will not forgive us (Matthew 6:15). This can quickly become one of the most challenging mandates we have received from God, considering how painful some of life's situations can be. But regardless of what we have endured, we must choose to obey Jesus and do the will of the Father and forgive, just as Jesus did when He laid down His life for us on the cross so we could be forgiven of our sins. We must never forget what Jesus warned us about the sin of unforgiveness: "But if ye forgive not men their trespasses, neither will your Father forgive your trespasses" (Matthew 6:15).

Even though forgiving a wrong may feel or seem impossible, when we understand the power of grace that Jesus won for us on the cross, we can choose to fall on Jesus, who will strengthen us and give us the supernatural ability to forgive! We cannot do this in our own strength or willpower, because some things that happen in life are just too painful! But glory to God, we can call on the name of Jesus, and He will come running to our sides in our times of need. Jesus promises to never leave us or forsake us (Deuteronomy 31:6). And He will not leave us comfortless: "I will not leave you comfortless: I will come to you" (John 14:18).

Choosing to obey the Father as Jesus did and forgive ourselves and others is a sign that we are fully mature in our faith! Sadly, one of the hardest things we will ever do in life is accept and believe by faith that we are truly forgiven of our sins. I love the story in Luke 7 in which the sinful woman, who was a prostitute, pushes her way in, breaking into the chamber where Jesus is dining with religious men who were leaders of their day. She refuses to be removed from the room and instead throws herself at the feet of Jesus and begins washing His feet with her hair and her tears. This woman knew she was a sinner, but she also knew in her heart that Jesus was the Messiah. She believed by faith that if she could honor Him by washing His dirty feet with her hair and tears, He would have mercy on her. She risked her life in doing this, but she was compelled by her heart of faith to risk everything to receive her freedom and healing. This is what radical faith looks like! When we are willing to lose everything to be set free, we will encounter Jesus and be healed.

> And, behold, a woman in the city, which was a sinner, when she knew that Jesus sat at meat in the Pharisee's house, brought an alabaster box of ointment, And stood at his feet behind him weeping, and began to wash his feet with tears, and did wipe them with the hairs of her head, and kissed his feet, and anointed them with the ointment. Now when the Pharisee which had bidden him saw it, he spake within himself, saying, This man, if he were a prophet, would have known who and what manner of woman this is that toucheth him: for she is a sinner. And Jesus answering said unto him, Simon, I have somewhat to say unto thee. And he saith, Master, say on. There was a certain creditor which had two debtors: the one owed five hundred pence, and the other fifty. And when they had nothing to pay, he frankly forgave them both. Tell me therefore, which of them will love him most? Simon answered and said, I suppose that he, to whom he forgave most. And he said unto him, Thou hast rightly judged. And he turned to the woman, and said unto Simon, Seest thou this woman? I entered

into thine house, thou gavest me no water for my feet: but she hath washed my feet with tears, and wiped them with the hairs of her head. Thou gavest me no kiss: but this woman since the time I came in hath not ceased to kiss my feet. My head with oil thou didst not anoint: but this woman hath anointed my feet with ointment. Wherefore I say unto thee, Her sins, which are many, are forgiven; for she loved much: but to whom little is forgiven, the same loveth little. (Luke 7:37–47)

What a stunning demonstration of the love of Jesus. He is so magnificent! He is so kind, loving, and full of mercy and grace. Remember that the woman had to force her way into the room where Jesus was because the religious leaders did not want her there. This breaks my heart! I believe we should make it easy for broken people to come to Jesus and be healed, and that we should never make it hard for people to enter into the presence of the Lord.

Regarding this issue, Jesus says the following in Mark 2:17: "When Jesus heard it, he saith unto them, They that are whole have no need of the physician, but they that are sick: I came not to call the righteous, but sinners to repentance."

What would happen if churches became more like "hospitals" for the "sick"—for people enslaved to sin who need healing—than places for "righteous" people to gather? The truth is that we have all, at one time, been sinners, and we have all fallen short of the glory of God (Romans 3:23). Titus 3:3–7 says it best:

> **For we ourselves also were sometimes foolish, disobedient, deceived, serving divers lusts and pleasures, living in malice and envy, hateful, and hating one another. But after that the kindness and love of God our Saviour toward man appeared, Not by works of righteousness which we have done, but according to his mercy he saved us, by the washing of regeneration, and renewing of the Holy Ghost; Which he shed on us abundantly through Jesus Christ our**

Saviour; That being justified by his grace, we should be made heirs according to the hope of eternal life.

It is imperative that we heed the warning Jesus gave in Mark 11:26 (NKJV): "But if you do not forgive, neither will your Father in heaven forgive your trespasses."

Faith and Forgiveness Lead to Freedom!

We will never be free until we choose to be loosed from unforgiveness by the power of the blood of Jesus and His great grace! How can we possibly be effective witnesses for Jesus Christ, sharing testimony of how grateful we are that His grace and mercy have forgiven us of our sin, and then, in a spirit of unforgiveness, turn around and slander, gossip, and in essence "kill" or destroy the reputation of someone who has offended or harmed us because we won't forgive *them* (1 John 4:20; James 3:9–10)? This is not the will of God! Jesus tells us in Scripture that vengeance belongs to *Him* and that *He* will fight our battles! If someone has harmed you, the Lord tells us to "turn the other cheek," and if someone takes your coat, we are to give him the other one also (Matthew 5:38–40). What I am describing to you may sound *radical*—because it *is* radical. The truth is that no one can forgive an offender by his or her own willpower or strength, but only by and through the grace and power of Jesus Christ.

The greatest victory in your life will come from learning that forgiveness is your "secret weapon" that defeats the demonic assignment on your life and sets you free so you can truly be a voice that gives glory to Jesus! Once you learn how powerful and healing it is to truly forgive others, you will find spiritual warfare coming to a screeching halt in your life! Hallelujah! If you desire to be used by God in the Kingdom, release all unforgiveness and bitterness in your heart and *be free*. If you are hungry for the anointing of God upon your life, forgive and be free! If you are believing for breakthrough and favor upon your life, choose today to forgive all offenses and be set free in Jesus's name!

I have come to understand that unforgiveness is like a cancer eating away at our spiritual lives. In reality, we are locking ourselves into a cage of bondage when we say the words, "I will never forgive them for what they did!" We will never truly walk in freedom and joy until we understand that everything in life boils down to being able to forgive as Jesus has forgiven us. In scripture, Jesus told the disciples that if they did not forgive others, their Father in heaven would not forgive them: "For if ye forgive men their trespasses, your heavenly Father will also forgive you: But if ye forgive not men their trespasses, neither will your Father forgive your trespasses" (Matthew 6:14–5).

Why is it so grievous to our Father in heaven when we will not forgive? We see clearly why in this widely known and loved verse: "For God so loved the world, that he gave his only begotten Son, that whosoever believeth in him should not perish, but have everlasting life" (John 3:16).[82]

From this verse, we see that God loved us enough to send His Son, Jesus Christ, to save us from our sins. Through Jesus, the ultimate sacrifice, we have received the full forgiveness of the Father by grace through faith. Let us pause for a moment and feel the gravity of what God is saying to us in His work in our hearts. When scripture says, "If you do not forgive, then my Father in heaven will not forgive you," the Lord Jesus is saying to us that He chose to obey the Father and lay down His life for us so that we could be forgiven of our sins, restored, and healed! If we turn and say to God, "No, I won't forgive someone else for what he or she did to me—it's unforgivable," then we are denying the same grace and faith that saved us. The unforgivable sin is to withhold forgiveness, because it rejects the salvation by grace that God has freely offered you, me, and all other people. The long and short of it is this: to refuse to forgive is to choose death rather than life! So I ask you to ask yourself, "Why would I choose to remove the blessings of God from my life because of unforgiveness?"

Beloved of the Lord, this is not our portion! Our portion is to prosper, gladness, the oil of joy, abundance, favor, and the blessings of God! But

---

[82]   See Romans 5:8: "But God commendeth his love toward us, in that, while we were yet sinners, Christ died for us." See also Isaiah 9:6: "For unto us a child is born, unto us a son is given: and the government shall be upon his shoulder: and his name shall be called Wonderful, Counsellor, The mighty God, The everlasting Father, The Prince of Peace."

none of this can be available to us—and we will never truly be free—until we choose to forgive all offences done to us. Let us choose to let go of offences and move forward, trusting all the details to Jesus. After all, Jesus is the only one who truly knows our hearts, and He is the only one worthy to judge our hearts, weighing out all the details. It is not our place to judge another person's heart. We do not have the right to say, "I can't forgive you," because saying this is actually the same as judging your brother or your sister. In fact, the real emotion or intent behind such a statement is pride and the hardening of your heart. Remember what happened to Pharaoh when he hardened his heart (Exodus 8:32; 9:12)?

Does Forgiving Mean Forgetting?

When we do not forgive, we wrongly put ourselves in the judgment seat over others. We cannot be the judge, because we are not God! Only God can truly test and judge a person's heart. It is our responsibility to forgive every time an offence comes, immediately forgiving the offender so we do not give the enemy a foothold (Ephesians 4:27). Forgiveness does not mean that we are required to forget everything that happened and jump right back into the middle of relationship with that person. That could dangerously position us to open the door wide for this person to create new trouble for us. No, that would not be wise! We can and should implement healthy boundaries when someone has crossed the line and caused harm. That way we can stand on God's Word and hold to the integrity of a healthy relationship while keeping our hearts clean from unforgiveness and leaving room for a genuine reconciliation of the relationship if that person chooses to change!

Truly forgiving means that we allow ourselves to cooperate with God's command to forgive. Let us choose, from our hearts, to live out the following declarations in Jesus's name:

1. I choose by faith to fall at the feet of Jesus, receiving His grace, and I declare my freedom from all torment, regret, fear, and pain from past offences.

2. I choose to refuse to retaliate or seek revenge, and I will not seek to destroy the reputation of the offender through gossip, slander, or evil-speaking.
3. I choose to show grace to others and declare, "Thank you, God, for delivering me from evil. Father, forgive them, for they do not know what they are doing" (see Luke 23:34).
4. I choose to focus on and be grateful for Jesus's forgiveness of my sins.
5. I choose to honor Jesus and help others to forgive, defeating triangulation and every form of manipulation and witchcraft, in Jesus's name.

Defeat the Devil: Choose to Forgive!

Pride will always tell you not to forgive. This is the plan of Satan, who wants to keep you bound. We overcome this snare of the enemy when we recognize that our pride must die so we can live for Christ. We cannot be proud and humble at the same time. Scripture tells us that God resists the proud: "But he giveth more grace. Wherefore he saith, God resisteth the proud, but giveth grace unto the humble" (James 4:6). Now notice the next verse: "Submit yourselves therefore to God. Resist the devil, and he will flee from you" (James 4:7). We need to resist all pride and submit ourselves to God so we can receive the grace we need in order to forgive. The Word clearly lays out the plan of action and the result:

1. Submit to God.
2. Resist the devil.
3. The devil will flee from you.

Victory! When we finally submit to God and resist the devil, we gain the ultimate victory. I love defeating the devil! As we obey God, He will cleanse and purify our hearts and enable us to resist double-mindedness and hypocrisy (see James 4:8). Only through surrendering our lives to the Lordship of Jesus Christ will we ever have true victory over sin! One of the most damaging sin patterns we see in our world today is self-idolatry. Do not fall into Satan's trap, but resist the devil and cry out to Jesus, who is mighty, to save, heal and restore you:

Draw nigh to God, and he will draw nigh to you. Cleanse your hands, ye sinners; and purify your hearts, ye double minded. (James 4:8)

Be sober, be vigilant; because your adversary the devil, as a roaring lion, walketh about, seeking whom he may devour ... (1 Peter 5:8)

Be sober-minded; be watchful. Your adversary the devil prowls around like a roaring lion, seeking someone to devour. (1 Peter 5:8 ESV)[83]

If we are honest, we will all admit that we have sinned and are not able to live perfect lives. We will never truly be at peace with ourselves or others until we learn to choose to obey the Lord Jesus by following His example of forgiveness.

Pray with me:

Father, in the name of Jesus Christ, I ask You to open our eyes and give us all a deeper revelation of relationship with You that is born out of surrender, grace, love, and mercy, and that You would seal this revelation by the power of Your Holy Spirit so that we will never neglect or forget the importance of forgiveness. May we never be trapped in that terrible sin of unforgiveness when You came to bring us home to live with You in heaven! Lord, help us by giving us the grace to trust You more. Cleanse us with Your blood and release the power of Your anointing to flow through us so that we may operate with the same grace and love You have given to us freely. Then we may truly be free, in Jesus's name. Amen!

FOURTEEN

"Come to Me"

And the Spirit and the bride say, Come. And let him that
heareth say, Come. And let him that is athirst come. And
whosoever will, let him take the water of life freely.
—Revelation 22:17

I have come to understand that in the matters of life, the bigger the
mess, the deeper the healing and deliverance that will come. Jesus
does not call us "beloved" because we've been so very righteous or
good or holy. Jesus calls us "beloved" because we have been branded
by the fiery furnace of life and trials and have chosen to follow Him.
This is what it means to belong to Him. The truth is that the greater the
brokenness, the more God's glory shines through us.

In Revelation 22:17, we hear the invitation to anyone who is thirsty
to come and take the water of life *freely*, or at no charge. We see this
again elsewhere:

> And he said unto, me, It is done. I am Alpha and Omega,
> the beginning and the end. I will give unto him that
> is athirst of the fountain of the water of life freely.
> (Revelation 21:6)

> Ho, every one that thirsteth, come ye to the waters,
> and he that hath no money; come ye, buy, and eat; yea,
> come, buy wine and milk without money and without
> price. (Isaiah 55:1)

Now let's look at the cross-reference verses from Isaiah 55:1:

> But whosoever drinketh of the water that I shall give him shall never thirst; but the water that I shall give him shall be in him a well springing up into everlasting life. (John 4:14)

> In the last day, that great day of the feast, Jesus stood and cried, saying, If any man thirst, let him come unto me, and drink. (John 7:37)

In John 4:14, Jesus is sitting by Jacob's well and asks a Samaritan woman to draw Him some water. The Samaritan woman is taken aback, because in that day no Jew would speak to a Samaritan, let alone a Samaritan *woman*, because Samaritans were despised for worshipping pagan gods and intermingling in marriage with Gentiles. But as the woman was drawing water from Jacob's well, Jesus said the following to her: "If thou knewest the gift of God, and who it is that saith to thee, Give me to drink; thou wouldest have asked of him, and he would have given to thee living water" (John 4:10).

Jesus has given us all an invitation to come to Him and drink deeply of His love so we will be satisfied and fulfilled. All that is required is to come and drink and receive His love! His arms are wide open to you—ready to receive you and set you free.

My Sheep Hear My Voice

The goodness of God and His plan for us is made clear in scripture: Once we belong to God through faith in Jesus Christ and the sealing power of the Holy Spirit, no one can snatch us from the Father's hand if we will *hear his voice* and *obey His Word*. The good news is, God gives us power through the infilling of the Holy Spirit to obey his voice when we truly belong to Him:

> But ye believe not, because ye are not of my sheep, as I said unto you. My sheep hear my voice, and I know

them, and they follow me:[84] And I give unto them eternal life; and they shall never perish, neither shall any man pluck them out of my hand. My Father, which gave them me, is greater than all; and no man is able to pluck them out of my Father's hand. I and my Father are one. (John 10:26–30)

In John 17, we see further confirmation of God's love for His sheep that He has given to Jesus to shepherd:

As thou hast given him power over all flesh, that he should give eternal life to as many as thou hast given him. (John 17:2)[85]

I have manifested thy name unto the men which thou gavest me out of the world: thine they were, and thou gavest them me; and they have kept they word. (John 17:6)

While I was with them in the world, I kept them in thy name: those that thou gavest me I have kept, and none of them is lost, but the son of perdition; that the scripture might be fulfilled. (John 17:12)

Father, I will that they also, whom thou hast given me, be with me where I am; that they may behold my glory, which thou hast given me: for thou lovedst me before the foundation of the world. (John 17:24)[86]

---

[84] See John 10:4, 14: "And when he putteth forth his own sheep, he goeth before them, and the sheep follow him: for they know his voice ... I am the good shepherd, and know my *sheep*, and am known of mine."

[85] See John 6:37, 39: "All that the Father giveth me shall come to me; and him that cometh to me I will in no wise cast out ... And this is the Father's will which hath sent me, that of all which he hath given me I should lose nothing, but should raise it up again at the last day."

[86] See 1 Thessalonians 4:17: "Then we which are alive *and* remain shall be caught up together with them in the clouds, to meet the Lord in the air: and so shall we ever be with the Lord."

If any man serve me, let him follow me; and where I am, there shall also my servant be: if any man serve me, him will my Father honour. (John 12:26)[87]

And if I go and prepare a place for you, I will come again, and receive you unto myself; that where I am, there ye may be also. (John 14:3)

Now more than ever, we must choose to believe the Word of God and hold on to Jesus with all our hearts because Jesus is coming back for His people! Scripture tells us that those who belong to Him by faith, will be caught up with Him in glory when He appears before all creation, coming upon the clouds with glory, and that those who believe in Him will be caught up to meet Him in the air: "Then we which are alive and remain shall be caught up together with them in the clouds, to meet the Lord in the air: and so shall we ever be with the Lord" (1 Thessalonians 4:17).

Truly, our King Jesus is coming for His beautiful bride!

The Harvest Is Now!

The harvest is here! It is now time to spread the good news of the gospel! Jesus is calling His people to enlist in His end-time army to win souls to Him before His return! This is the will of the Father: that we share the gospel with people so they may know Jesus Christ and be saved! This was the final instruction Jesus gave to His disciples while He was with them, instructing them for forty days after His resurrection and before His ascension back to the Father:

Say not ye, There are yet four months, and then cometh harvest? behold, I say unto you, Lift up your eyes, and look on the fields; for they are white already to harvest. (John 4:35)

---

[87]   See Matthew 16:24: "Then said Jesus unto his disciples, If any *man* will come after me, let him deny himself, and take up his cross, and follow me."

And he said unto them, Go ye into all the world, and preach the gospel to every creature. He that believeth and is baptized shall be saved; but he that believeth not shall be damned. And these signs shall follow them that believe; In my name shall they cast out devils; they shall speak with new tongues; They shall take up serpents; and if they drink any deadly thing, it shall not hurt them; they shall lay hands on the sick, and they shall recover.[88] So then after the Lord had spoken unto them, he was received up into heaven, and sat on the right hand of God.[89] (Mark 16:15–9)

Jesus's final request to His apostles before He ascended back to the Father in heaven was to commission every believer to share the good news of the gospel with the world. Hypothetically speaking, if you knew that *you* were about to leave your life and your loved ones on this earth, I imagine your final words would most likely reflect the deepest desires and expressions of your heart to your loved ones before your departure. This leads us to ask ourselves, "What is my greatest desire?" We must ask ourselves, "Do I want what I want, or do I want what *God* wants?"

We know from scripture that the greatest desire of Jesus was that we would fulfill the will of God, just as He did, winning souls to the Kingdom of God: "For I came down from heaven, not to do mine own will, but the will of him that sent me" (John 6:38).

Jesus's love, mercy and grace were demonstrated in His willingness to fulfill the plans and purposes of the Father in obedience and to lay down His life for His friends that we might live (John 15:13). His

---

[88] See James 5:14: "Is any sick among you? let him call for the elders of the church; and let them pray over him, anointing him with oil in the name of the Lord."

[89] See Acts 1:2: "Until the day in which he was taken up, after that he through the Holy Ghost had given commandments unto the apostles whom he had chosen." See also Acts 1: 9–11: "And when he had spoken these things, while they beheld, he was taken up; and a cloud received him out of their sight. And while they looked stedfastly toward heaven as he went up, behold, two men stood by them in white apparel; Which also said, Ye men of Galilee, why stand ye gazing up into heaven? this same Jesus, which is taken up from you into heaven, shall so come in like manner as ye have seen him go into heaven."

blood, shed on the cross for us, opened the door to our freedom in Him forevermore. What would have happened if Jesus had rebelled and said no to God the Father? I am so grateful that Jesus obeyed the will of the Father in laying down His life for us on the cross! What better way is there to show our gratitude to Jesus than to pick up our sickle and enlist in the great end time harvest of souls for God's glory? Scripture tells us that the field is ripe and ready for harvest, but the laborers are few. I believe that it is the will of God for every believer to win souls to Christ and that everyone is called to "minister" the love of Jesus to others. This is the will of the Father—that not one soul would be lost!

> And this is the Father's will which hath sent me, that of all which he hath given me I should lose nothing, but should raise it up again at the last day. And this is the will of him that sent me, that every one which seeth the Son, and believeth on him, may have everlasting life: and I will raise him up at the last day.[90] (John 6:39–40)

> And I give unto them eternal life; and they shall never perish, neither shall any man pluck them out of my hand. (John 10:28)

> While I was with them in the world, I kept them in thy name: those that thou gavest me I have kept, and none of them is lost, but the son of perdition: that the scripture might be fulfilled. (John 17:12)

---

[90] See John 6:27, 47, 54: "Labour not for the meat which perisheth, but for that meat which endureth unto everlasting life, which the Son of man shall give unto you: for him hath God the Father sealed ... Verily, verily, I say unto you, He that believeth on me hath everlasting life ... Whoso eateth my flesh, and drinketh my blood, hath eternal life; and I will raise him up at the last day." See also John 3:15–16: "That whosoever believeth in him should not perish, but have eternal life. For God so loved the world, that he gave his only begotten Son, that whosoever believeth in him should not perish, but have everlasting life." See also John 4:14: "But whosoever drinketh of the water that I shall give him shall never thirst; but the water that I shall give him shall be in him a well of water springing up into everlasting life."

In Mark 16, we see undeniably that it is the will of the Father that we, as believers, go into the world and share the gospel—that we live out the Great Commission to bring many souls into the Kingdom of God through faith in Jesus Christ for salvation. We read previously in John 6 that it is the will of the Father that Jesus would lose "none of all those [the Father] has given [Him]" (NIV), and we see His promise that "neither shall any man pluck them out of my hand." This is the Father's *will for us*. We must cooperate with His will for it to come to pass. We must seek to obey the Father just as Jesus did and walk through whatever fiery trials come, knowing that the Lord is faithful to us and that He will not let us fall. Psalm 91 is a beautiful passage that many people pray for protection from the enemy. I see this protection not as a mantra to quote when we are fearful, but as a banner of love over us. As a result of our relationship with Jesus and the authority we have in Christ, we can rest because we are protected by His blood and are in covenant with Him!

He that dwelleth in the secret place of the most High shall abide under the shadow of the Almighty.[91] I will say of the LORD, He is my refuge and my fortress: my God; in him will I trust.[92] Surely he shall deliver thee from the snare of the fowler, and from the noisome pestilence.[93] He shall cover thee with his feathers, and under his wings shalt thou trust: his truth shall be thy shield and buckler.[94] Thou shalt not

---

[91]   See Psalm 27:5: "For in the time of trouble he shall hide me in his pavilion: in the secret of his tabernacle shall he hide me; he shall set me up upon a rock." See also Psalm 32:7: "Thou *art* my hiding place; thou shalt preserve me from trouble; thou shalt compass me about with songs of deliverance. Selah." See also Isa. 32:2: "And a man shall be as an hiding place from the wind, and a covert [shelter] from the tempest; as rivers of water in a dry place, as the shadow of a great rock in a weary land."

[92]   See Psalm 142:5: "I cried unto thee, O LORD: I said, Thou *art* my refuge *and* my portion in the land of the living."

[93]   See Psalm 124:7: "Our soul is escaped as a bird out of the snare of the fowlers: the snare is broken, and we are escaped."

[94]   See Psalm 17:8: "Keep me as the apple of the eye, hide me under the shadow of thy wings."

be afraid for the terror by night; nor for the arrow that flieth by day;[95] Nor for the pestilence that walketh in darkness; nor for the destruction that wasteth at noonday. A thousand shall fall at thy side, and ten thousand at thy right hand; but it shall not come nigh thee. Only with thine eyes shalt thou behold and see the reward of the wicked.[96] Because thou hast made the LORD, which is my refuge, even the most High, thy habitation; There shall no evil befall thee, neither shall any plague come nigh thy dwelling.[97] For he shall give his angels charge over thee, to keep thee in all thy ways.[98] They shall bear thee up in their hands, lest thou dash thy foot against a stone. Thou shalt tread upon the lion and adder [cobra]: the young lion and the dragon [serpent] shalt thou trample under feet. Because he hath set his love upon me, therefore will I deliver him: I will set him on high, because he hath known my name.[99] He shall call upon me, and I will answer him: I will be with him in trouble; I will

---

95   See Isaiah 43:2: "When thou passest through the waters, I *will be* with thee; and through the rivers, they shall not overflow thee: when thou walkest through the fire, thou shalt not be burned; neither shall the flame kindle upon thee."

96   See Psalm 37:34: "Wait on the LORD, and keep his way, and he shall exalt thee to inherit the land: when the wicked are cut off, thou shalt see *it*." See also Malachi 1:5: "And your eyes shall see, and ye shall say, The LORD will be magnified from the border of Israel."

97   See Proverbs 12:21: "There shall no evil happen to the just: but the wicked shall be filled with mischief."

98   See Psalm 34:7: "The angel of the LORD encampeth round about them that fear him, and delivereth them." See also Matthew 4:6: "And saith unto him, If thou be the Son of God, cast thyself down: for it is written, He shall give his angels charge concerning thee: and in *their* hands they shall bear thee up, lest at any time thou dash thy foot against a stone." See also Luke 4:10: "For it is written, He shall give his angels charge over thee, to keep thee."

99   Note that the narrative in verse 14 changes from third person to first person to personalize God's word of encouragement to *you*!

deliver him, and honour him.[100] With long life will I satisfy him, and shew him my salvation. (Psalm 91:1–16)

> Hear these words resounding deep within your spirit: "With long life will I satisfy him, and shew him my salvation." How beautiful are the love, grace, peace, joy, and satisfaction that come from truly knowing Jesus through a personal encounter with Him! It is really so very simple, and people can overcomplicate it. Knowing Jesus is about loving Him because He first loved us (1 John 4:19) and simply resting in the truth that He will never, ever stop loving us. It is my humble prayer that you will give your heart to Jesus today and begin to enjoy all of His benefits (Psalm 103) now and forevermore in Jesus's name. Amen!

Psalm 103

Bless the LORD, O my soul: and all that is
within me, bless his holy name.
Bless the LORD, O my soul, and forget not all his benefits:
Who forgiveth all thine iniquities; who healeth all thy diseases;
Who redeemeth thy life from destruction; who crowneth
thee with lovingkindness and tender mercies;
Who satisfieth thy mouth with good things; so
that thy youth is renewed like the eagle's.
The LORD executeth righteousness and
judgment for all that are oppressed.
He made known his ways unto Moses, his
acts unto the children of Israel.

---

[100]   See Psalm 50:15: "And call upon me in the day of trouble: I will deliver thee, and thou shalt glorify me." See also Isaiah 43:2: "When thou passest through the waters, I will be with thee; and through the rivers, they shall not overflow thee: when thou walkest though the fire, thou shalt not be burned; neither shall the flame kindle upon thee."

The LORD is merciful and gracious, slow to
anger, and plenteous in mercy.
He will not always chide: neither will he keep his anger for ever.
He hath not dealt with us after our sins; nor
rewarded us according to our iniquities.
For as the heaven is high above the earth, so great is his
mercy [lovingkindness] toward them that fear him.
As far as the east is from the west, so far hath
he removed our transgressions from us.
Like as a father pitieth his children, so the
LORD pitieth them that fear him.
For he knoweth our frame; he remembereth that we are dust.
As for man, his days are as grass: as a flower
of the field, so he flourisheth.
For the wind passeth over it, and it is gone; and
the place thereof shall know it no more.
But the mercy of the LORD is from everlasting to everlasting upon
them that fear him, and his righteousness unto children's children;
To such as keep his covenant, and to those that
remember his commandments to do them.
The LORD hath prepared his throne in the
heavens; and his kingdom ruleth over all.
Bless the LORD, ye his angels, that excel in strength, that do
his commandments, hearkening unto the voice of his word.
Bless ye the LORD, all ye his hosts; ye
ministers of his, that do his pleasure.
Bless the LORD, all his works in all places of his
dominion: bless the LORD, O my soul. (Psalm 103)

Hallelujah!
All hail King Jesus!
Amen!

Your Identity in Christ: The Blessings of Salvation

According as he hath chosen us in him before the foundation of the world, that we should be holy and without blame before him in love: Having predestinated us unto the adoption of children by Jesus Christ to himself, according to the good pleasure of his will, To the praise of the glory of his grace, wherein he hath made us accepted in the beloved.
—Ephesians 1:4–6

As believers in Jesus Christ, we have been adopted into the family of God and now are called chosen, adopted, redeemed, fathered, sealed, and enlightened carriers of God's glory!

1. **We Are Chosen and Predestined (Ephesians 1:5–6)**

   [5] "Having predestinated us unto the adoption of children by Jesus Christ to himself, according to the good pleasure of his will ..." (Acts 13:48; John 1:12; 1 Corinthians 1:21)

   [6] "To the praise of the glory of his grace, wherein he hath made us accepted in the beloved."
   a. **Acts 13:48**: "And when the Gentiles heard this, they were glad, and glorified the word of the Lord: and as many as were ordained to eternal life believed." (Acts 2:47)

i.   **Acts 2:47**: "Praising God, and having favour with all the people. And the Lord added to the church daily such as should be saved." (Acts 5:14)

ii. **Acts 5:14**: "And believers were the more added to the Lord, multitudes both of men and women."

b.   **John 1:12**: "But as many as received him, to them gave he power to become the sons of God, even to them that believe on his name."

c.   **1 Corinthians 1:21**: For after that in the wisdom of God the world by wisdom knew not God, it pleased God by the foolishness of preaching to save them that believe." (Daniel 2:20)

i.   **Daniel 2:20**: "Daniel answered and said, Blessed be the name of God for ever and ever: for wisdom and might are his." (Matthew 6:13; Romans 11:33)

1.   **Matthew 6:13** "And lead us not into temptation, but deliver us from evil: For thine is the kingdom, and the power, and the glory, for ever. Amen."

2.   **Romans 11:33**: "O the depth of the riches both of the wisdom and knowledge of God! how unsearchable are his judgments, and his ways past finding out!"

2.   **Redemption by the Blood of Jesus (Ephesians 1:7–12)**

[7] "In whom we have redemption through his blood, the forgiveness of sins, according to the riches of his grace ..." (Hebrews 9:12)

a.   **Hebrews 9:12**: "Neither by the blood of goats and calves, but by his own blood he entered in once into the holy place, having obtained eternal redemption for us." (Hebrews 10:4; Isaiah 53:12)

i.   **Hebrews 10:4**: "For it is not possible that the blood of bulls and of goats should take away sins" (Micah 6:6–7)

1.   **Micah 6:6, 7** "Wherewith shall I come before the LORD, and bow myself before the high God? shall I come before him with burnt offerings, with calves of a year old? Will the Lord be pleased with thousands of rams, or with ten thousands of rivers of oil? shall I give my

firstborn for my transgression, the fruit of my body for the sin of my soul?"

    ii. **Isaiah 53:12**: "Therefore will I divide him a portion with the great, and he shall divide the spoil with the strong; because he hath poured out his soul unto death: and he was numbered with the transgressors; and he bare the sin of many, and made intercession for the transgressors." (Psalm 2:8; Mark 15:28)

        1. **Psalm 2:8**: "Ask of me, and I shall give thee the heathen for thine inheritance, and the uttermost parts of the earth for thy possession."

        2. **Mark 15:28**: "And the scripture was fulfilled, which saith, And he was numbered with the transgressors."

[8] "Which he lavished upon us, in all wisdom and insight …"

[9] "Having made known unto us the mystery of his will, according to his good pleasure which he hath purposed in himself:"

[10] "That in the dispensation of the fulness of times he might gather together in one all things in Christ, both which are in heaven, and which are on earth; even in him …" (Ephesians 3:15; 2:9; Colossians 1:16, 20)

[11] "In whom also we have obtained an inheritance, being predestinated according to the purpose of him who worketh all things after the counsel of his own will." (Romans 8:17; Isaiah 46:10)

a. **Romans 8:17**: "And if children, then heirs; heirs of God, and joint-heirs with Christ; if so be that we suffer with him, that we may be also glorified together."

b. **Isaiah 46:10**: "Declaring the end from the beginning, and from ancient times the things that are not yet done, saying, My counsel shall stand, and I will do all my pleasure." (Psalm 33:11; Acts 5:39; Hebrews 6:17)

    i. **Psalm 33:11**: "The counsel of the LORD standeth for ever, the thoughts of his heart to all generations."

ii. **Acts 5:39**: "But if it be of God, ye cannot overthrow it; lest haply ye be found even to fight against God."

iii. **Hebrews 6:17**: "Wherein God, willing more abundantly to shew unto the heirs of promise the immutability of his counsel, **confirmed** it by an **oath.**"

[12] "That we should be to the praise of his glory, who first trusted in Christ." (2 Thessalonians 2:13)

a. **2 Thessalonians 2:13**: "But we are bound to give thanks alway to God for you, brethren beloved of the Lord, because God hath from the beginning chosen you to salvation through sanctification of the Spirit and belief of the truth."

3. **Fathered into the Family of God (Ephesians 1:10)**

[10] "That in the dispensation of the fulness of times he might gather together in one all things in Christ, both which are in heaven, and which are on earth; even in him ..." (Ephesians 3:15; Philippians 2:9; Colossians 1:16, 20)

a. **Ephesians 3:15**: "Of whom the whole family in heaven and earth is named."

b. **Philippians 2:9**: "Wherefore God also hath highly exalted him, and given him a name which is above every name." (Hebrews 2:9; Acts 2:33; Ephesians 1:21)

i. **Hebrews 2:9**: "But we see Jesus, who was made a little lower than the angels for the suffering of death, crowned with glory and honour; that he by the grace of God should taste death for every man." (Isaiah 53:12)

ii. **Acts 2:33**: "Therefore being by the right hand of God exalted, and having received of the Father the promise of the Holy Ghost, he hath shed forth this, which ye now see and hear." (Acts 5:31; Psalm 68:18; Philippians 2:9)

iii. **Ephesians 1:21**: "Far above all principality, and power, and might, and dominion, and every name that is named, not only in this world, but also in that which is to come:"

c. **Colossians 1:16, 20**: "For by him were all things created, that are in heaven, and that are in earth, visible and invisible, whether they be thrones, or dominions, or principalities, or powers: all things were created by him, and for him [John 1:3; Hebrews 1:2, 3] ... And, having made peace through the blood of his cross, by him to reconcile all things unto himself; by him, I say, whether they be things in earth, or things in heaven." (Romans 5:1; Ephesians 2:14)

i.   **Romans 5:1**: "Therefore being justified by faith, we have peace with God through our Lord Jesus Christ."

ii. **Ephesians 2:14**: "For he is our peace, who hath made both one, and hath broken down the middle wall of partition between us."

4. **Sealed to God (Ephesians 1:13–14, 17–18)**

[13] "In whom ye also trusted, after that ye heard the word of truth, the gospel of your salvation: in whom also after that ye believed, ye were sealed with that holy Spirit of promise ..." (John 1:17)

a.   **John 1:17**: "For the law was given by Moses, but grace and truth came by Jesus Christ."

[14] "Which is the earnest of our inheritance until the redemption of the purchased possession, unto the praise of his glory." (2 Corinthians 5:5)

a.   **2 Corinthians 5:5**: "Now he that hath wrought us for the selfsame thing is God, who also hath given unto us the earnest of the Spirit."

[17] "That the God of our Lord Jesus Christ, the Father of glory, may give unto you the spirit of wisdom and revelation in the knowledge of him." (Romans 15:6; Colossians 1:9)

a.   **Romans 15:6**: "That ye may with one mind and one mouth glorify God, even the Father of our Lord Jesus Christ."

b.   **Colossians 1:9**: "For this cause we also, since the day we heard it, do not cease to pray for you, and to desire that ye might be filled with the knowledge of his will in all wisdom and spiritual understanding."

[18] "The eyes of your understanding being enlightened; that ye may know what is the hope of his calling, and what the riches of the glory of his inheritance in the saints." (2 Corinthians 4:6; Hebrews 6:4; Ephesians 2:12)

5. **The Glory of His Inheritance (Ephesians 1:18)**

[18] "The eyes of your understanding being enlightened; that ye may know what is the hope of his calling, and what the riches of the glory of his inheritance in the saints." (2 Corinthians 4:6; Hebrews 6:4; Ephesians 2:12)

a. **2 Corinthians 4:6**: "For God, who commanded the light to shine out of darkness, hath shined in our hearts, to give the light of the knowledge of the glory of God in the face of Jesus Christ." (Genesis 1:3; Isaiah 9:2; 2 Peter 1:19)

   i. **Genesis 1:3**: "And God said, Let there be light: and there was light."

   ii. **Isaiah 9:2**: "The people that walked in darkness have seen a great light: they that dwell in the land of the shadow of death, upon them hath the light shined." (Matthew 4:16; Luke 1:79)

   iii. **2 Peter 1:19**: "We have also a more sure word of prophecy; whereunto ye do well that ye take heed, as unto a light that shineth in a dark place, until the day dawn, and the day star arise in your hearts." (John 8:34)

      1. **John 8:34**: "Jesus answered them, Verily, verily, I say unto you, Whosoever committeth sin is the servant of sin."

b. **Hebrews 6:4**: "For it is impossible for those who were once enlightened, and have tasted of the heavenly gift, and were made partakers of the Holy Ghost." (John 4:10; Ephesians 2:8; Hebrews 2:4)

   i. **John 4:10**: "Jesus answered and said unto her, If thou knewest the gift of God, and who it is that saith to thee, Give me to drink; thou wouldest have asked of him, and he would have given thee living water."

   ii. **Ephesians 2:8**: "For by grace are ye saved through faith; and that not of yourselves: it is the gift of God."

iii. **Hebrews 2:4**: "God also bearing them witness, both with signs and wonders, and with divers miracles, and gifts of the Holy Ghost, according to his own will." (Acts 2:22)

1. **Acts 2:22**: "Ye men of Israel, hear these words; Jesus of Nazareth, a man approved of God among you by miracles and wonders and signs, which God did by him in the midst of you, as ye yourselves also know." (Isaiah 50:5; John 3:2; 5:6)

   - **Isaiah 50:5**: "The Lord GOD hath opened mine ear, and I was not rebellious, neither turned away back." (Psalm 40:6)

   - **Psalm 40:6**: "Sacrifice and offering thou didst not desire; mine ears hast thou opened: burnt offering and sin offering hast thou not required." (Psalm 51:16; Isaiah 1:11; Jeremiah 6:20; 7:22–23)

   - **Psalm 51:16**: "For thou desirest not sacrifice; else would I give it: thou delightest not in burnt offering."

   - **Isaiah 1:11**: "To what purpose is the multitude of your sacrifices unto me? saith the LORD: I am full of the burnt offerings of rams, and the fat of fed beasts; and I delight not in the blood of bullocks, or of lambs, or of he goats."

   - **Jeremiah 6:20**: "To what purpose cometh there to me incense from Sheba, and the sweet cane from a far country? your burnt offerings are not acceptable, nor your sacrifices sweet unto me."

   - **Jeremiah 7:22, 23**: "For I spake not unto your fathers, nor commanded them in the day that I brought them out of the land of Egypt, concerning burnt offerings or sacrifices: But this thing commanded I them, saying, Obey my voice, and I will be your God, and ye shall be my people: and walk ye in all the ways that I have commanded you, that it may be well unto you."

   - **John 3:2**: "The same came to Jesus by night, and said unto him, Rabbi, we know that thou art a teacher come from God: for no man can do these miracles that thou doest, except God be with him."

- **John 5:6**: "When Jesus saw him lie, and knew that he had been now a long time in that case, he saith unto him, Wilt thou be made whole?"

c. **Ephesians 2:12**: "That at that time ye were without Christ, being aliens from the commonwealth of Israel, and strangers from the covenants of promise, having no hope, and without God in the world."

6. **Glory Carries by the Holy Spirit's Power (Ephesians 1:19–23)**

¹⁹ "And what is the exceeding greatness of his power to us-ward who believe, according to the **working of his mighty power,**"

²⁰ "Which he wrought in Christ, when he raised him from the dead, and set him at his own right hand in the heavenly places,"

²¹ "Far above all principality, and power, and might, and dominion, and every name that is named, not only in this world [age], but also in that which is to come:"

²² "And hath put all things under his feet, and gave him to be the head over all things to the church." (Psalm 8:6; 1 Corinthians 15:27; Hebrews 2:7)

a. **Psalm 8:6**: "Thou madest him to have dominion over the works of thy hands; thou hast put all things under his feet."

b. **1 Corinthians 15:27**: "For he hath put all things under his feet. But when he saith all things are put under him, it is manifest that he is excepted, which did put all things under him."

c. **Hebrews 2:7**: "Thou madest him a little lower than the angels; thou crownedst him with glory and honour, and didst set him over the works of thy hands."

²³ "Which is his body, the fulness of him that filleth all in all."

The Parable of the Ten Virgins
(Matthew 25:1–13)

[1] "Then shall the kingdom of heaven be likened unto ten virgins, which took their lamps, and went forth to meet the bridegroom." (Ephesians 5:29, 30; Revelation 19:7; 21:2, 9)

a. **Ephesians 5:29–30:** "For no man ever yet hated his own flesh; but nourisheth and cherisheth it, even as the Lord the church: For we are members of his body, of his flesh, and of his bones." (Genesis 2:23)

b. **Revelation 19:7:** "Let us be glad and rejoice, and give honour to him: for the marriage of the Lamb is come, and his wife hath made herself ready." (Luke 12:36; John 3:29; Ephesians 5:23, 32)

c. **Revelation 21:2, 9:** "And I John saw the holy city, new Jerusalem, coming down from God out of heaven, prepared as a bride adorned for her husband [Isaiah 52:1; Hebrews 11:10; Isaiah 54:5] ... And there came unto me one of the seven angels which had the seven vials full of the seven last plagues, and talked with me, saying, Come hither, I will shew thee the bride, the Lamb's wife."

[2] "And five of them were wise, and five were foolish." (Matthew 13:47; 22:10)

a. **Matthew 13:47**: "Again, the kingdom of heaven is like unto a net, that was cast into the sea, and gathered of every kind." (Matthew 22:9–10)

b. **Matthew 22:10**: "So those servants went out into the highways, and gathered together all as many as they found, both bad and good: and the wedding was furnished with guests." (Matthew 13:38, 47–48; Acts 28:28)

[3] "They that were foolish took their lamps, and took no oil with them:"

[4] "But the wise took oil in their vessels with their lamps."

[5] "While the bridegroom tarried, they all slumbered and slept." (1 Thessalonians 5:6)
a. **1 Thessalonians 5:6**: "Therefore let us not sleep, as do others; but let us watch and be sober." (Matthew 25:5, 13)

[6] "And at midnight there was a cry made, Behold, the bridegroom cometh; go ye out to meet him."

[7] "Then all those virgins arose, and trimmed their lamps."

[8] "And the foolish said unto the wise, Give us of your oil; for our lamps are gone out."

[9] "But the wise answered, saying, Not so; lest there be not enough for us and you: but go ye rather to them that sell, and buy for yourselves."

[10] "And while they went to buy, the bridegroom came; and they that were ready went in with him to the marriage: and the door was shut." (Luke 13:25)
a. **Luke 13:25**: "When once the master of the house is risen up, and hath shut to the door, and ye begin to stand without, and to knock at the door, saying, Lord, Lord, open unto us; and he shall answer and say unto you, I know you not whence ye are." (Isaiah 55:6; Revelation 22:11; Luke 6:46; Matthew 7:23
    i. **Isaiah 55:6**: "Seek ye the LORD while he may be found, call ye upon him while he is near." (Matthew 5:25; John 7:34)

   ii. **Revelation 22:11** "He that is unjust, let him be unjust still: and he which is filthy, let him be filthy still: and he that is righteous, let him be righteous still: and he that is holy, let him be holy still."

   iii. **Luke 6:46**: "And why call ye me, Lord, Lord, and do not the things which I say?" (Malachi 1:6; Matthew 7:21; 25:11)

[11] "Afterward came also the other virgins, saying, Lord, Lord, open to us." (Matthew 7:21–23)

a. **Matthew 7:21**: "Not everyone that saith unto me, Lord, Lord, shall enter into the Kingdom of Heaven; but he that doeth the will of my Father which is in heaven. (Hosea 8:2)

   i. **Hosea 8:2**: "Israel shall cry unto me, My God, we know thee."

b. **Matthew 7:22** "Many will say to me in that day, Lord, Lord, have we not prophesied in thy name? [Numbers 24:4] and in thy name have cast out devils? and in thy name done many wonderful works?" (Operating in gifts does not mean you have a personal relationship with Jesus by faith unto good works!)

c. **Matthew 7:23**: "And then will I profess unto them, I never knew you: depart from me, ye that work iniquity."

[12] "But he answered and said, Verily I say unto you, I know you not." (Psalm 5:5; Habakkuk 1:13; John 9:31)

a. **Psalm 5:5**: "The foolish shall not stand in thy sight; thou hatest all workers of iniquity." (Habakkuk 1:13; Psalm 1:5)

b. **Habakkuk 1:13**: "Thou art of purer eyes than to behold evil, and canst not look on iniquity: wherefore lookest thou upon them that deal treacherously, and holdest thy tongue when the wicked devoureth the man that is more righteous than he?"

c. **John 9:31**: "Now we know that God heareth not sinners: but if any man be a worshipper of God, and doeth his will, him he heareth."

[13] "Watch therefore, for ye know neither the day nor the hour wherein the Son of man cometh." (1 Thessalonians 5:6; Matthew 24:36, 42)

a. **1 Thessalonians 5:6**: "Therefore let us not sleep, as do others; but let us watch and be sober." (Matthew 25:5; 13)

b. **Matthew 24:36, 42**: "But of that day and hour knoweth no man, no, not the angels of heaven, but my Father only [Mark 13:32; Acts 1:7; Zechariah 14:7] ... Watch therefore: for ye know not what hour your Lord doth come." (Luke 21:36; 1 Thessalonians 5:6)

   i. **Zechariah 14:7**: "But it shall be one day which shall be known to the LORD, not day, nor night: but it shall come to pass, that at evening time it shall be light." (Matthew 24:36; Isaiah 30:26)

   ii. **Luke 21:36**: "Watch ye therefore, and pray always, that ye may be accounted worthy to escape all these things that shall come to pass, and to stand before the Son of man." (Mark 13:33; Luke 18:1; 20:35)

BE FREE

WITH *Ashley Gronholm*

BROADCAST NOW AVAILABLE TO 195 NATIONS ON THE BE FREE APP

APPLE TV • ROKU • YOUTUBE

Magdala School of Apostolic Ministry

A unique one-year Bible training and ordination program designed to equip believers and lay ministers in the Word of God so they may fully receive the pure anointing of Jesus Christ by the power of the Holy Spirit and by His grace!

Register online at www.BeFreeInChrist Ministry.org/Bible-Training/

Find Ashley Gronholm's music on Apple Music, Spotify, and all other listening platforms!

Stay Connected!
Download our free app, now available in the App Store and the Google Play Store! Find us also on Roku TV and Apple TV.

Apple App Store

Google Play Store